COUNTED
SASHIKO
EMBROIDERY

Other Schiffer Craft Books on Related Subjects:

Juno's Nature Embroidery Notebook: Stitching Plants, Animals, and Stories, Juno, ISBN 978-0-7643-6422-8

Whitework Embroidery: Designs and Accessories with a Modern Twist, Seiko Nakano, ISBN 978-0-7643-6423-5

Retro Cross Stitch: 500 Patterns, French Charm for Your Stitchwork, Véronique Enginger, ISBN 978-0-7643-5479-3

Library of Congress Control Number: 2022951483

Produced by BlueRed Press Ltd. 2023
Designed by Insight Design Concepts Ltd.
Type set in Montserrat

ISBN: 978-0-7643-6673-4
Printed in China

Published by Schiffer Craft
An imprint of Schiffer Publishing, Ltd.
4880 Lower Valley Road
Atglen, PA 19310
Phone: (610) 593-1777; Fax: (610) 593-2002
Email: Info@schifferbooks.com
Web: www.schifferbooks.com

For our complete selection of fine books on this and related subjects, please visit our website at www.schifferbooks.com. You may also write for a free catalog.

Schiffer Publishing's titles are available at special discounts for bulk purchases for sales promotions or premiums. Special editions, including personalized covers, corporate imprints, and excerpts, can be created in large quantities for special needs. For more information, contact the publisher.

We are aways looking for people to write books on new and related subjects. If you have an idea for a book, please contact us at proposals@schifferbooks.com.

COUNTED
SASHIKO
EMBROIDERY

31 Projects with 80 Kogin and 200 Hishizashi Patterns

Keiko Sakamoto

SCHIFFER
CRAFT

4880 Lower Valley Road • Atglen, PA 19310

Contents

Introduction

I still remember when I saw a pair of work pants so completely covered with hishizashi that the underlying cloth was no longer visible. The impression I got from that motivates me to this day in my work on counted sashiko embroidery.

Kogin and hishizashi began as a way to strengthen cloth and make it warmer in a punishing environment, and within the strict sumptuary restrictions imposed by the ruling clans. I think those poverty-stricken Japanese farmers did their embroidery truly out of necessity, stitching intently and using the limited materials available to them to clothe their families.

The beauty of kogin and hishizashi lies in the regularity that comes from counting the threads in the weave. By sticking to that discipline, kogin and hishizashi have maintained a universal and wholesome beauty that still fascinates us in the modern era.

What would those women of old think if they knew that the embroidery they made in their corner of the north country has crossed the sea and been introduced to the world? I think that they would be, as I am, very happy to know that it has become a handicraft that brightens the lives of many people in unknown lands.

This book is dedicated to the anonymous women of the north country who created this embroidery in times past.

Respectfully and prayerfully,
Keiko Sakamoto

Two Kinds of Embroidery

The Birth of Two Kinds of Embroidery

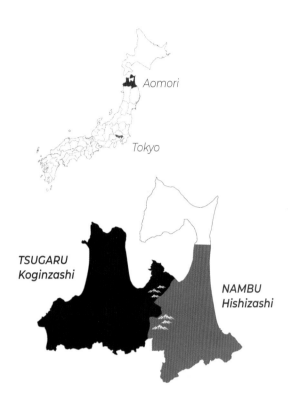

TSUGARU
Koginzashi

NAMBU
Hishizashi

in the summer. Spinning it into thread continued every evening in the fall, and those threads were at last set on the loom in the winter. In this way, one bolt of cloth was produced. Given that the cloth still had to be dyed with indigo before it was ready to use, one can imagine how much work went into it and how precious the resulting fabric was. However, it was not suitable clothing for a northern climate, because hemp cloth is not very warm and its fibers break easily. At some point, sashiko embroidery was applied for reinforcement and insulation, and that later developed into beautiful geometric patterns.

It is not known for certain when those geometric patterns were first applied to kimonos, but there are some records in the old sources. In 1788, Sadahiko Hirano, a retainer of the Tsugaru clan, recorded an embroidered kimono in *Oumin Zui*, an illustrated encyclopedia of rural folk. From this, it can be deduced that this counted embroidery was already established by the middle of the eighteenth century.

Both kogin and hishizashi were born at the northern tip of the Japanese island of Honshu, in what is now Aomori Prefecture. In the Edo period (1603–1868), the Tsugaru clan ruled the part to the west of the central Ou mountain range, facing the Sea of Japan, and the Nambu clan ruled the eastern part, which faces the Pacific Ocean. Owing to differences in geography and climate, very different cultures and languages grew in these two regions. Similarly, the peasants who lived there created distinctive styles of counted embroidery for their clothing.

At that time, the clans' policy was to encourage agriculture and conserve food, clothing, and housing, emphasizing self-sufficiency. Since cotton did not grow in the Tsugaru and Nambu regions at the cold, northern tip of Honshu, and cotton imports from other clans were restricted, the only material available to the peasants for their clothing was the hemp and ramie that they grew for themselves. They would sow seeds at the edge of the fields in the spring, then harvest the hemp and extract the fiber

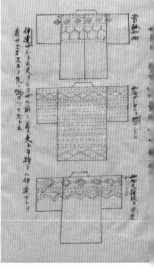

Oumin Zui describes the life—clothes, food, and shelter—of ordinary people in Tsugaru, in sketches and explanatory text. To the left is a farmer wearing a kogin kimono. On the right are the types of kogin embroidery of that time.

e Geography of the Two Regions

e natural environments are quite different between the
ugaru region in the west and the Nambu region to its
st, and the lives of the people differed accordingly.
e Tsugaru region was more prosperous since it could
ow rice, which was at the time used in place of currency.
cause they raised one rice crop each year, the Tsugaru
ople's lives had a regular, annual rhythm. When it came
embroidery, they planned out the overall design, which
luded complicated patterns, for a well-thought-out
d beautiful structure. Also, they disdained to embroider
users that would get covered in mud from the rice
ddies, and focused their energies on gorgeous designs
the upper halves of their kimonos.

The Nambu region, on the other hand, has less snow than
its western neighbor but is cooled by a cold wind—the
Yamase—in the summer and consequently could not grow
rice. Instead, the people there grew various subsistence
field crops, including pulses, wheat, millet, buckwheat, and
vegetables. It is thought that the Nambu people decorated
their trousers and aprons because they worked mostly
in dry fields. It could be that the relatively faster rhythm
of dry-field farming led to the technique of stacking up
embroidery blocks like bricks.

If we reflect on the patterns in this light, kogin begins to
resemble the straight, regular lines of rice paddies, while
hishizashi takes on the appearance of fields planted with
patches of various crops, one next to the other.

Characteristics of the Two Styles

TSUGARU
Koginzashi

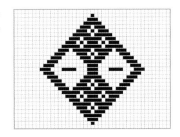

NAMBU
Hishizashi

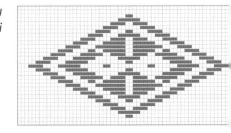

The patterns use odd numbers of threads. Shift one over with each row.

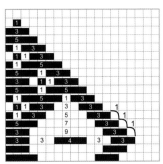

The patterns use even numbers of threads. Shift two over with each row.

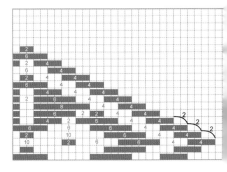

The width is equal to the height.

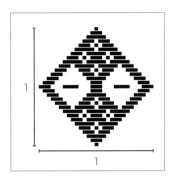

The width is double the height.

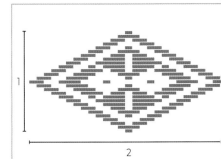

Surround the pattern with multiple borders.

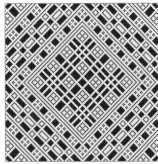

Stack the patterns in rows.

White cotton floss on dark indigo cloth

White/dark-blue cotton floss or multicolored woolen yarn on pale indigo cloth

Decline and Revival

hen Japan entered the Meiji era (1868–1912), cotton
read, which had hitherto been scarce, was suddenly easy
come by. Furthermore, in 1891 a railroad from Tokyo to
omori brought colorful yarns from overseas. The middle
eiji period was the peak for both kogin and hishizashi.
any of the beautiful garments that are left today were
ade around that time. Toward the end of the Taisho
ign (1912–1926), the availability of cheap cotton cloth
ed women from the labor of weaving and embroidering
mp cloth and led to the demise of kogin and hishizashi
broidery.

uneyoshi Yanagi, founder of the folk crafts revival in the
rly part of the Showa reign (1926–1989), reevaluated
e beauty of these styles and featured them in volume
of the journal *Kogei* (Handicrafts), praising them as
e epitome of regional handicraft." It was then that
gin and hishizashi, which had been work wear for the
asants of Japan's northernmost extremity, first became
own to the world. That sparked a local movement to
vive and preserve them, and the Hirosaki Kogin Institute
s supported this revival until the present day. The first
ector of the institute, Naomichi Yokoshima, focused
collecting literature and cataloging patterns, learning
e techniques from the last generation to make the
broidery. His diligent efforts at recording bore fruit with
r six hundred patterns preserved at the institute.

The patterns were reevaluated after World War II, thanks to
the efforts of Chuzaburo Tanaka, a folklorist born in Aomori
Prefecture. In his twenties, he independently researched
the Ainu of the Shimokita Peninsula and excavated
Jomon sites. Starting in 1965, he expanded his focus from
archeology to include ethnology and folk art and spent the
next forty years in fieldwork, listening to tales of past times
from the old men and women in the villages.

From early on, Tanaka looked at materials remaining in the
Aomori area, beginning with the old cloth (known as *Boro*)
that had been passed down for generations in farming
families, questioning villages and farmhouses throughout
the region. He paid special attention to collecting examples
of hishizashi and researching its patterns, and his book
Nambu Tsuzure Hishizashi Moyoshu ("A Nambu Hishizashi
pattern collection"), is extremely valuable as one of only
a few books on hishizashi. Tanaka's enormous collection
of clothing and tools, amounting to some 20,000 items,
includes 786 embroidered kimonos from Tsugaru/Nambu
that are designated as a national heritage (Important
Tangible Folk-Culture Property). A 520-item collection of
hemp cloth and spinning tools is similarly designated by
Aomori Prefecture.

Nambu Tsuzure Hishizashi Moyoshu
A Nambu Hishizashi pattern collection"
s a compilation of hishizashi patterns
urveyed by Chuzaburo Tanaka.

About four hundred hishizashi patterns are
shown.

Historical Examples of the Two Styles

Counted sashiko embroidery was originally for work clothes
and was born out of the harsh lives of women living in
the frigid north country. In the eighteenth century (Edo
period), when cloth was precious, it began among peasants
as a technology that was necessary in their lives.

Kogin Kimono
*Hemp/cotton, Tsugaru region
(Aomori Prefecture), Meiji era
(nineteenth century), National
Museum of Ethnology, Osaka*

Front
*A geometric pattern is precisely
embroidered with white cotton
thread on dark indigo cloth.*

reached its zenith toward the end of the nineteenth
ntury (Meiji era) but quickly declined at the beginning
the twentieth century (Taisho era) as transport networks
veloped. Now it is preserved only in museums. The
lowing are pictures of some of the precious remaining
amples.

k

*back of the body has the
tern called a "horse's bit," which
the meaning of an amulet that
ents evil from entering from
back when walking on a path
ugh a field.*

Hishizashi Kimono

*Hemp/cotton, Nambu region (Aomori Prefecture), Meiji era
(nineteenth century), Japan Folk Crafts Museum, Tokyo*

Back

*The back of the body and sleeves are
embroidered with numerous diamond patterns.
It was said that they were eyes for the back and
that the corners of the diamonds ward off evil.*

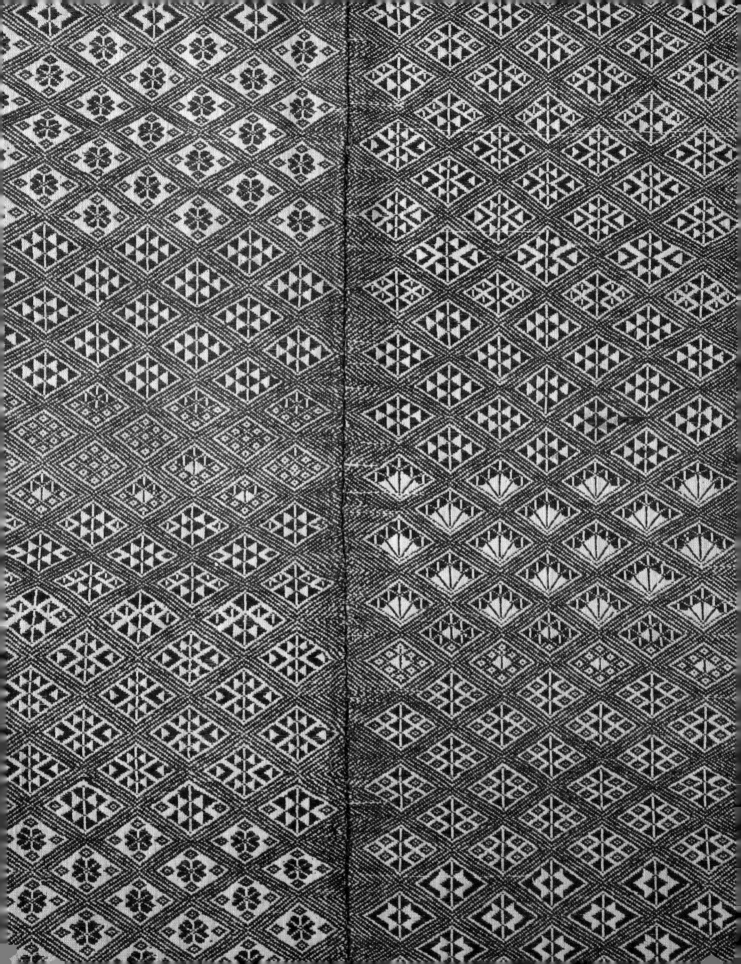

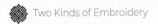

Hishizashi Tattsuke *(work pants)*
Hemp/cotton, Nambu region (Aomori Prefecture), Meiji-Taisho era
(twentieth century), National Museum of Ethnology, Osaka (Clothing and
Accessory Collection Database created by the MCD project)

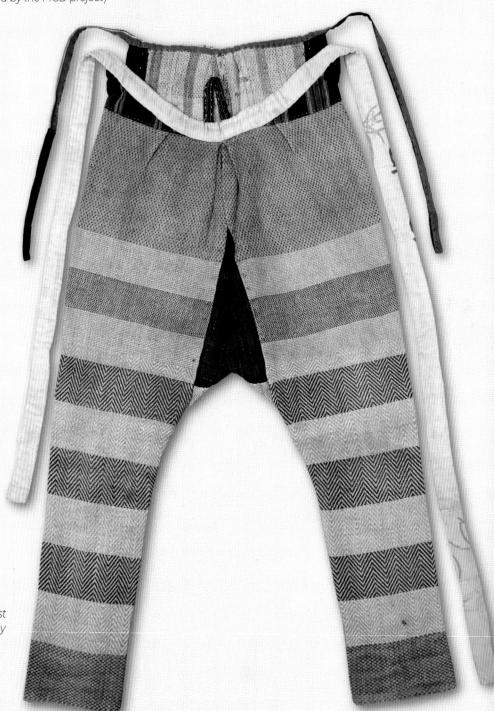

Front
Tattsuke were women's work clothes, indispensable for work in the fields and forests. In order to protect against insects and thorns, they were carefully embroidered until the weave was no longer visible.

Back
Only in the Nambu region were insulation, reinforcement, and decoration applied to pants. Cloth has been added to the back, and it is tailored three-dimensionally for ease of movement.

19

Hishizashi Maekake (apron)
Hemp/cotton/wool, Nambu region (Aomori Prefecture), Taisho era (twentieth century), National Museum of Ethnology, Osaka (Clothing and Accessory Collection Database created by the MCD project)

Front

The center part of each (opposite and above) is made of embroidered hemp cloth, and both sides are sewn together with dark-blue cotton cloth. Printed cloth was used for the strings. Maekake were worn when going out or selling goods, but not when working in the fields.

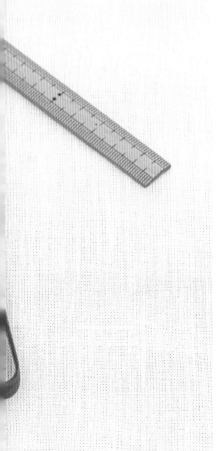

BASIC
PATTERNS
AND
TECHNIQUES

Patterns

The Basic Kogin Patterns

There are about forty traditional kogin patterns, which are called *modoko*. They are given names from plants, animals, and insects; farms and fields; nature; and daily life. Adding the diminutive "*ko*" to the end of cute things—such as *hanako* and *mameko*—is a characteristic of the northern dialects. Kogin surrounds these basic patterns with multiple layers of diagonal, continuous, or border patterns to expand them and build a comprehensive pattern.

Japanese	English
Kacharazu	The reverse of *mameko*
Hanako	Flower
Mameko	Bean
Musubibana	Four *hanako* together
Urokogata	Fish scales (small)
Shimadazashi	Named after *shimadayui*, a popular hairstyle of the time
Fukube	Gourd
Komakurazashi	Little pillow—resembles the small, wooden pillows that were used at the time
Neko no ashi	Cat's paw
Neko no managu	Cat's eye
Tekonako	Butterfly
Kinone no kikurako	Wooden saddle made of a bent tree root
Mameko no yotsukogori	Fragments of ice
Urokogata	Fish scales (large)
Bekozashi	Ox
Uma no kutsuwa	A horse's bit (i.e., attached to a bridle)
Kurubikara	Walnut shell
Yotsumameko	Four beans
Yasukozashi	Trip-'em-up stitch
Ta no aze	Path through the rice paddies
Kogorizashi	Frozen stitch
Yabane	Arrow
Tomarazu	Endless
Sayagata	Key/fret—symbolizes the wish to live long and prosper
Kumozashi	Spider

The Basic Hishizashi Patterns

There are about four hundred traditional hishizashi patterns, which are called *katako*. Each of them is surrounded by a border called *ashigai*, which is shaped like a sideways diamond (rhombus). Just as in kogin patterns, they are symbolic representations of familiar plants and animals. Hishizashi is made by lining these patterns up in rows.

Japanese	English
Ume no hana	Plum blossom
Beko no kura	Pack saddle
Sorobandama	Abacus beads
Kiji no ashi	Pheasant's foot
Yabane	Arrow
Urokomon	Fish scale motif
Mitsubishi	Three diamonds
Yotsubishi	Four diamonds
Itsutsubishi	Five diamonds
Nanatsubishi	Seven diamonds
Kokonotsubishi	Nine diamonds
Nashi no monko	Pear motif
Ougi no monko	Fan motif
Ishidatami	Cobblestone
Ajiro	Wicker
Yanoha	Arrow fletching
Aishigemasu	Square boxes
Uma no managu	Horse's eye
Sobagarabishi	Buckwheat husk
Neko no managu	Cat's eye

Pattern Structure

How to Arrange the Patterns

At first glance, kogin embroidery appears very complicated. If you look carefully, however, you will see that it is made up of a few simple patterns. Many of the basic patterns come from combinations of a few small patterns such as *kacharazu*, *mameko*, and *hanako*.

If you just follow the basic kogin rule of counting odd numbers of threads when spacing stitches, you can combine or break up patterns in any way you like. Similarly with hishizashi, if you follow the rule of spacing by even numbers of threads, you can make the patterns larger or smaller.

Start by looking closely at each pattern, then try drawing it on graph paper. By practice drawing, you will become familiar with the patterns, and by following the basic rules, you will be able to arrange the patterns in your own way.

How to Expand Kogin Patterns

To expand the pattern, you can directly connect single patterns or put *ito-bashira* (thread column) or *ito-nagare* (thread flow) borders in between them. A thread column is a straight row of stitches. A thread flow is a diagonal row of stitches shifted over one each time. These two are essential for expanding kogin patterns.

Flows and Enclosures

These give kogin patterns their distinctive appearance. They connect single patterns with diagonal borders and expand them by wrapping around. A "flow" (dark blue in the chart) is the name for something that seamlessly connects patterns into a whole. An "enclosure" (light blue in the chart) wraps around four sides of the independent diamonds.

Right: *Elaborations on* Musubibana.

Opposite: *Examples of flows and enclosures.*

Materials

Fabrics

Since you will need to count the threads in the cloth as you embroider, you can use any plain cloth with threads that you can count. In this book, I have used both fabric made for kogin and linen fabric made for embroidery.

Thread count is given as the number of warp and weft threads per inch. In counted embroidery—where you count the number of threads to place the stitches—the size of the pattern varies depending on the cloth used. With a low-thread-count cloth, the pattern will be larger, and with a higher-thread-count cloth, the pattern will be smaller. The pictures below are actual size.

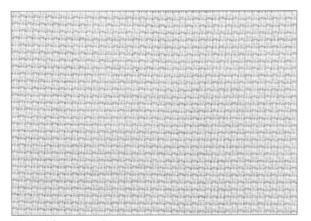

DMC Aida, cotton, 14 count

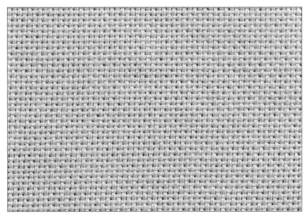

Olympus Congress, cotton, 18 count

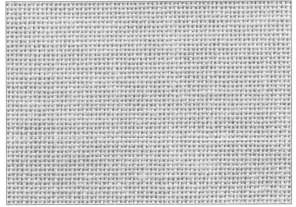

Vaupel & Heilenbeck linenband, linen, 22 count

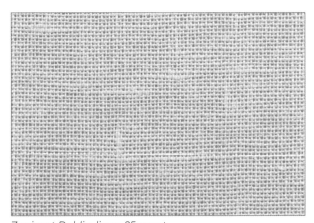

Zweigart Dublin, linen, 25 count

Effect of Weave on Patterns

The shape of the pattern can change depending on whether the cloth is an even weave or uneven weave. In Aomori's traditional kogin embroidery, a handwoven uneven weave (where there are more warp threads than weft threads per inch) has been used for a long time and is still made as cloth for kogin. If you use that cloth, the kogin patterns will come out as vertical diamonds, and hishizashi patterns will not be as wide.

Kogin even weave

Hishizashi even weave

Kogin uneven weave

Hishizashi uneven weave

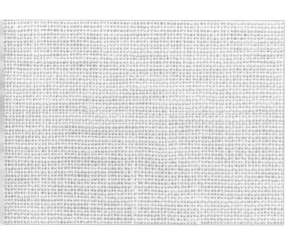

Zweigart Cashel, linen, 28 count

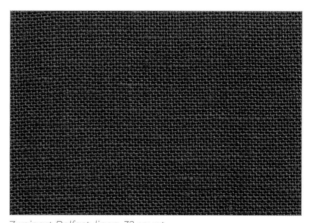

Zweigart Belfast, linen, 32 count

Tokiya Asa 252, linen and ramie, warp 20 x weft 18 count

Daruma kogin cloth, linen, warp 23 x weft 18 count

Threads

You may choose whichever threads you like, depending on the fineness of the weave or the texture that you want to create. Sashiko and kogin thread are matte, so they have a plain appearance. Sashiko thread is twisted more tightly than kogin thread, so it is easier to get a clean, even finish. On the other hand, the fluffier feel of kogin thread makes for a softer appearance. No. 25 embroidery thread has a glossy finish like silk and is available in many colors. You can also use a thin yarn in place of thread.

Ordinarily, the pattern stands out better if you use an embroidery thread that is a little thicker than the threads in the weave of the fabric. You can choose a thickness that you like, matching it to the weave.

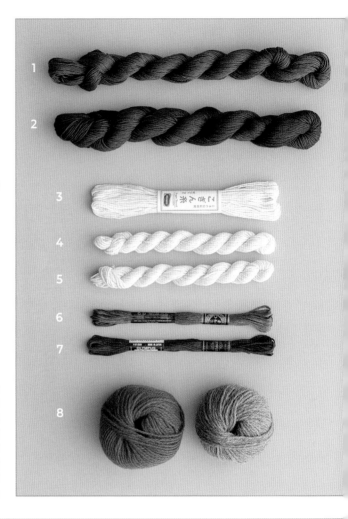

1. Six-strand sashiko thread
2. Eight-strand sashiko thread
3. Six-strand kogin thread (Olympus)
4. Eight-strand kogin thread
5. Ten-strand kogin thread
6. No. 25 embroidery thread (DMC)
7. No. 25 embroidery thread (Olympus)
8. Woolen yarn

Tip: To use the thread efficiently

a. Take off the label, untie it, and cut the knot.

b. Rewind on cardboard, or something similar. Cut off the length you need to use. It is handy to write the type of thread it is on the card, along with any other important details.

ʘols

ɪedles

ɪect a needle with a large hole for ease of threading.
ɪce you will be stitching between the yarns of the cloth,
ɪ a needle with a round tip that will not split the fibers.

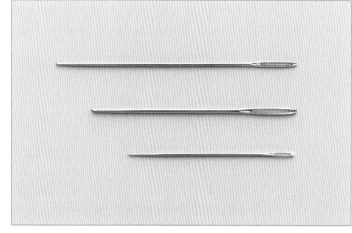

*From top to bottom: Kogin, tapestry, and
embroidery needles*

ɪher tools

ɪne more tools to make the work go more smoothly.

*From left to right: Graph paper—for making designs;
ruler—to decide where to start stitching; tailor's chalk—
for marking; antifraying liquid—apply to the edge of
cloth to prevent fraying; sewing scissors—for cutting
thread; dressmaker's scissors—for cutting fabric*

ɪip: Prevent fraying

ɪfter the cloth has been cut, the cut
ɪdges fray easily, so dealing with
ɪhis beforehand will make your work
ɪasier. Cut the cloth slightly larger
ɪhan needed, and either (a) apply
ɪn antifraying liquid or (b) hem the
ɪdges.

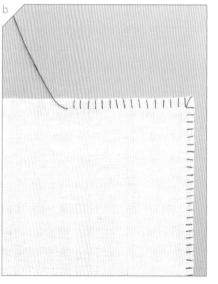

Techniques
How to Read the Charts

The way to read charts is the same for kogin and hishizashi. There are two types of chart styles for counted embroidery: the old style as used in this book, and the modern style. See the charts on the right: in the top chart, the threads in the warp or weft of the fabric are represented by the squares in the graph. In the lower chart, they are represented by lines. In both charts, the bold horizontal lines show where the embroidery floss goes across the front side of the fabric.

Both systems are based on the same basic principle of counting the warp threads in the fabric for each stitch (odd numbers for kogin, even for hishizashi), so choose whichever style you like. I have used square charts in this book.

How to Read the Templates

The templates to be found in the final section of the book (p. 97 onward) illustrate the patterns necessary to complete the projects in the book. Above each is the pattern's number referenced in the project section. The figures given in parentheses below each pattern indicate its size as the number of threads it spans on the cloth. There is only one number for kogin, since the height and width are the same. The numbers for hishizashi are width x height. Please use these as a reference when making your designs. Also identified are Japanese names. See pp. 25 and 27 for the English translations.

How to Stitch Single Patterns

The method of stitching is the same for kogin and hishizashi. Both styles are generally vertically or horizontally symmetrical, so we usually start from the center. Rotate the cloth 180 degrees after every row so that you always stitch in the same direction, and finish one half (top or bottom) at a time. Let's start learning the basics by stitching a kogin single pattern.

Square
Old chart pattern style as used in this book. This is the kogin pattern Tekonako (butterfly).

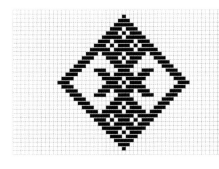

Line
New chart pattern style

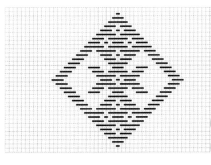

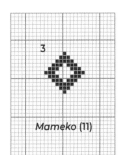

Above: *A basic kogin pattern, #3 Mameko (p. 98). It spans 11 threads.*

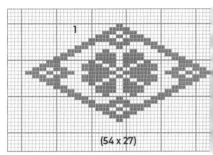

Above: *Hishizashi pattern #1 Ume no hana (p. 114) spans 54 threads wide by 27 high.*

This pattern is Bekozashi (the ox). Stitch the upper and lower halves, extending from the red line.

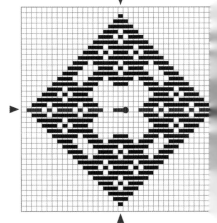

● *Start point*

Crease the cloth to give the center of the pattern.

Start with the stitch closest to the center of the pattern, putting the needle through from the back to the front.

Stitch the left half of the first row as shown in the pattern.

Pull the needle off the thread and rethread it on the other side.

Rotate the cloth 180 degrees and finish stitching the other half of the first row.

When you have finished stitching the first row, turn the cloth over.

Tug on the loose ends until they are the same length on both sides (do this only for stand-alone patterns).

Pull the center of the thread out about ⅛ in. (3 mm) with the tip of the needle.

While holding the ends of the stitching with both hands, pull the cloth diagonally, alternately to the left and right several times.

Repeat step 9 until the slack from step 8 is gone. This is called *ito-koki*.

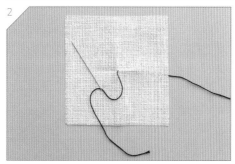

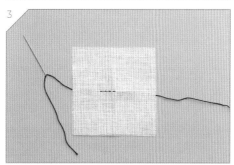

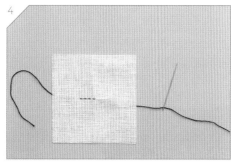

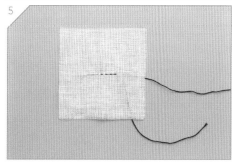

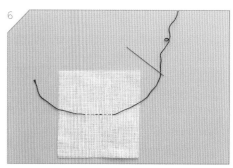

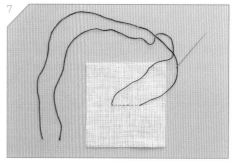

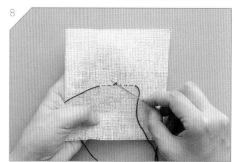

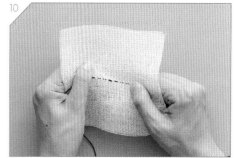

11. Turn the cloth back to the front side and stitch the second row. Using the first row as a guide, count the threads according to the pattern.

12. After finishing the second row

13. Leave a loop of thread about ⅛ in. (3 mm) between the first and second rows on the backside.

14. While firmly holding both ends of the stitching, pull the cloth diagonally to work the thread in (*ito-koki*).

15. Hold the slack from step 13 with your fingers. With the other hand, pinch the stitching between your thumb and forefinger and pull, rubbing both sides of the cloth as you do.

16. Turn the cloth back to the front side and stitch the third row. Repeat the *ito-koki* after every row.

17. Stitching the ninth row

18. Stitching the last row in the bottom half

19. Turn the cloth over and slowly pull the thread from the back to create a loop of about ⅛ in. (3 mm).

20. Pull the thread gently until the loop is the same size as the other rows.

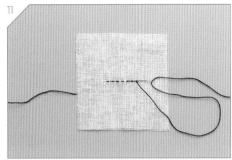
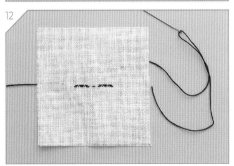
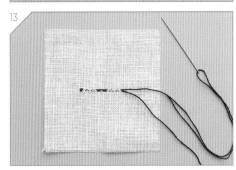
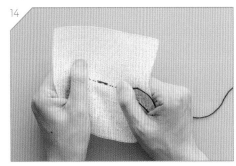
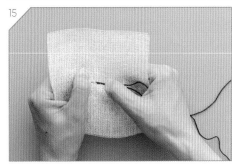
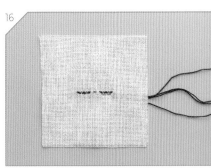

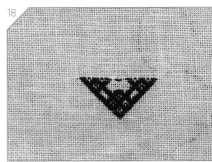
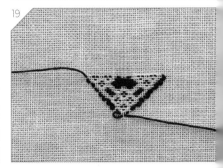
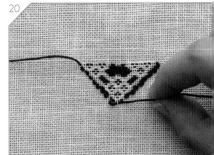

Pick up two warp threads from the previous row, skipping one in between them.

Rotate the cloth 180 degrees.

Gently pull the thread through to form a loop.

Continue to pull the thread slowly until the loop is the same size as the other rows.

Cut the end of the thread, leaving ⅛ to ¼ in. (3–5 mm).

Thread the needle on the other end and finish the other half in the same way.

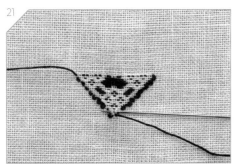

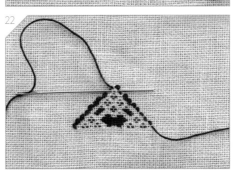

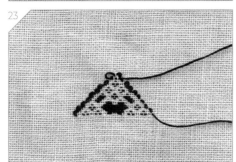

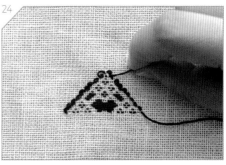

Tip: If the ends of the yarns get uneven . . .

a. Lower the needle down to the bottom.

b. Align the yarns before moving it back.

How to Stitch Continuous Patterns

Think of the centerline of the chart as the axis of
the continuous pattern and begin stitching from
the center of that line. Continuous patterns have
long horizontal runs, so use a longer piece of thread.
However, if it is too long, it can be damaged by
friction, so keep it under about 54 in. (137 cm) at
a time. Later in this chapter, I will explain how to
change threads when you run out in the middle and
how to clean up (finish off) the ends.

● *Start point*

This pattern is Fukube *(gourds) with a border.
Stitch the upper and lower parts, extending from
the red line.*

Mark the middle and the top of the cloth with a thread for reference. Start with the stitch closest to the center of the pattern, putting the needle through from the back to the front.

Stitch the left half of the first row as shown in the pattern.

Turn the cloth over and rethread the needle with the other end of the thread. Leave about 4 in. (10 cm) loose at the first end of the thread.

Turn the cloth back over again and finish stitching the rest of the first row.

The completed first row

The backside of the cloth

Pull the center of the thread out about ⅛ in. (3 mm) with the tip of the needle.

While holding the ends of the stitching with both hands, pull the cloth diagonally, alternately to the left and right several times.

Do this (ito-koki) until the slack in the center is reduced, letting the thread ease into the fabric. Ideally, the thread should appear to rest lightly on top of the flat cloth.

Turn the cloth to the front again and stitch the second row. Using the first row as a guide, count the threads according to the pattern.

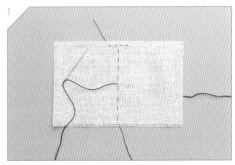

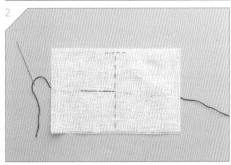

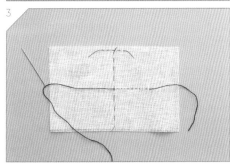

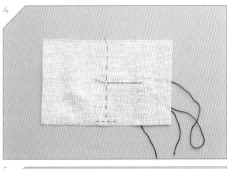

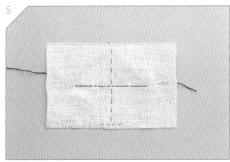

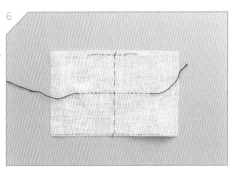

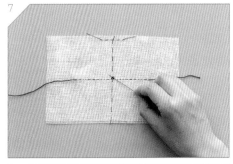

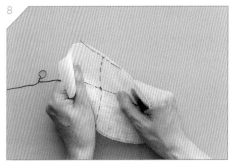

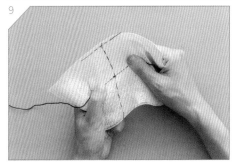

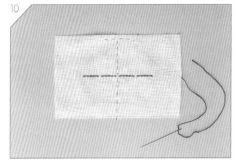

11. The back of the fabric after stitching the second row. When moving on to the next row, leave a ⅛ in. (3 mm) loop of loose thread in between.

12. While holding both ends of the stitching, pull the cloth diagonally to work the thread in (ito-koki).

13. Work the thread into the cloth well.

14. After finishing the third row

15. After finishing the fourth row. Proceed to the rest of the top half, flipping the cloth after each row.

16. When you get to the end of the thread, change to a new one. Always change threads on the backside of the cloth, on either the left or right end of a row. Start by picking up every other thread from the warp of the previous row.

17. Pick up these threads where they are behind a stitch and cannot be seen from the front. The overlap should be approximately ½ in. (1 cm).

18. About 4 in. (10 cm) at the end of the old thread should be enough to clean up (finish off) the end.

19. Rotate the cloth 180 degrees and pull the needle.

20. Continue to pull the thread slowly until the loop is the same size as the other rows.

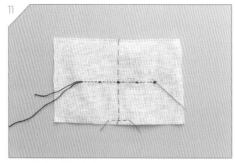

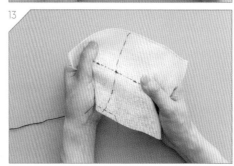
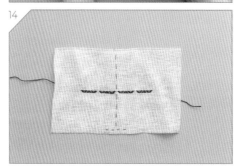
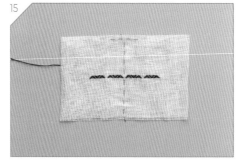

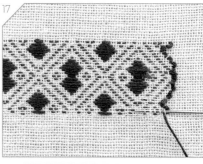

1. Cut the end of the thread, leaving ⅛–¼ in. (3–5 mm).

2. Thread the needle with a new thread and start stitching again from the side opposite where you just finished.

3. Turn the cloth over to the front and continue stitching. The loose end of the new thread should be tucked away in the same way as in steps 16–21.

4. Finish the rest in the same way.

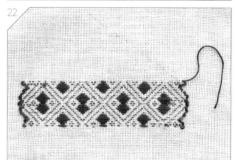

Tip: If the thread gets twisted while stitching . . .

If the yarns of the thread come untwisted while you are stitching, spin the needle to retwist it. Alternatively, if the thread becomes too tightly twisted, spin the needle in the opposite direction to loosen it. If you continue to stitch while thread is over- or undertwisted, the stitches will not come out even. Check the state of the thread from time to time and adjust it as you go.

Tip: *Ito-koki*

This is one of the most important things for making beautiful counted embroidery. It prevents the embroidery from getting lost in the weave or pulling on the fabric, and it helps make the stitches round and beautiful.

After stitching each row, turn the cloth over and pull some slack into the center (from the loose end), then tug the cloth diagonally several times. If you pull too much slack into the middle, you may not be able to get all of it out. In that case, pull on the thread until it is no longer loose.

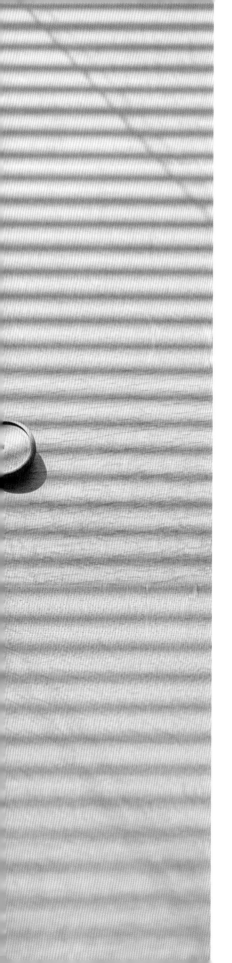

PROJECTS

ひっそりした町並の花道に、アサガオ、ヘチマ、茄子、キュウリ、サツマなどの苗、種
イモの露店が、あっちに二、三軒、こっちに三、四軒と、店をひらいている。
客の影もまばらに、食いもの店は、屋台のトウモロコシ売りが「一軒だけ」でている。
「鳩ケ谷の市って、サツマ苗、種イモのでる六月生亡で、ちかごろ夏場はさっぱりですわ。」
と、いう。ただし、十二月の暮の市は、昔そのままの賑わいだそうだ。

鳩ケ谷市の歴史は、古い。
永井伯順の『関東綺談』の冒頭に、将軍の日光御成街道で市を開くというのを、とくべつ御許しの書面
を得ていた。

徳川時代の中期に、鳩ケ谷のボロ市がでてくるが、それよりずっと昔、
市神さまの祠（上町と中町との境あたりにあるのを、やっとで見つけた。星棋に、パン
を起点にして、近在の農民たちの密で鳩ケ谷の市は、だんだん近在の
種もの・野菜苗の露店が、駅わってきた。
ペン幕が丈長い）を潜う店もまじり、
苗もの、古着・野良着・蒙魚屋・古本屋どれも並んで。
大正から昭和の初期（かけて鳩ケ谷の市は、
子ども相手には、アメ屋・ゴム風船・金魚屋・古本屋などと並んで、松井原水のゴム通し、ガイの
大正には、ハイイロ〇〇をひいて近行徒走ら試読

そのかわりに、駅の弘賃会と植木苗木商組合の共催で、東口広場に植木・苗木、鉢物の市が
開かれていた。駅の弘賃会と植木苗木商組合の共催で、
キューポラの街・川口市が、鋳物工業のほかに、はじめての試みという。──知らない人も多いらしい。
の安行地帯をかかえこんでいることは、知るひとぞ知る。もうひとつの顔、日本有数の植木苗木

川口の植木市

駅苗の植木市には、モミジ、ケヤキ、紅シダン、五葉松、ゴムノ木、シュロなどの苗木
や鉢もの、ツツジ、バラ、ハイビスカスなどの花卉盆栽など、一鉢（株）三〇〇円から七〇
〇一八〇〇円ほどの生産者価格で、たくさん並んでいる。
「安いな、安いな、なんで安いんだ」
血相をかえて、うろうろ見てまわるサラリーマンふうの男、買物かごの女、子どもをお

Bookmarks

Let's start by stitching a small, basic
kogin pattern. Using linen band for
embroidery, it is easy to make your own
original bookmark.

Finished size
6¾ x 1⅝ in. (17 x 4.2 cm)

Materials for each bookmark
6¾ in. (17 cm) of Vaupel & Heilenbeck linen band (raw
  linen), 1⅝ in. (4.2 cm) wide, 22 count
yd. (90 cm) of Olympus kogin thread
  (here, blue #343; those illustrated on p. 47, *left to right*,
  purple #655, blue #343, red #194, navy blue #335, and
  pink #166)

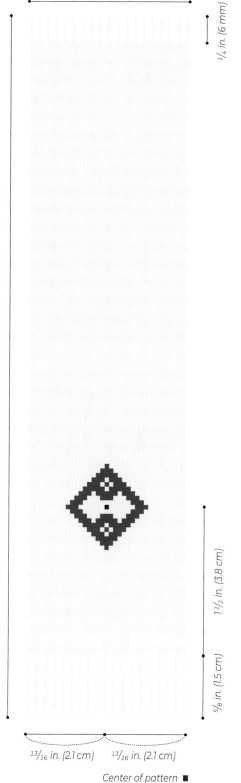

1⅝ in. (4.2 cm)

¼ in. (6 mm)

6¾ in. (17 cm)

1½ in. (3.8 cm)

⅝ in. (1.5 cm)

Right: *Kogin pattern #6* Shimadazashi

13/16 in. (2.1 cm)   13/16 in. (2.1 cm)

Center of pattern ■

1. Prepare a piece of linen tape 1⅝ in. (4.2 cm) wide by 6¾ in. (17 cm) long. Slowly pull out the weft threads to undo the weave until ⅝ in. (1.5 cm) of the warp is exposed.

2. Take the loose thread that you have pulled out and thread it onto the needle to hem the edge. Bring the thread from the back to the front, between the second and third warp threads from the right. Wrap around the first two weft threads and come out the back.

3. Repeat, moving two threads to the left each time, making a fringe.

4. Cut the ends to even up the length of the fringe.

5. Make a ¼ in. (6 mm) fringe on the upper edge in the same way.

6. Stitch the pattern so that the center is 1½ in. (3.8 cm) above the bottom edge.

7. Double up a piece of the embroidery floss and pass it through near the upper edge of the cloth.

8. Tie the thread and cut to an appropriate length.

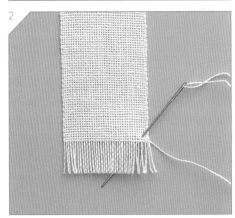

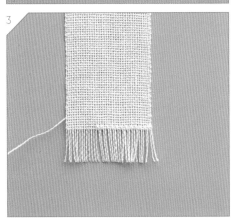

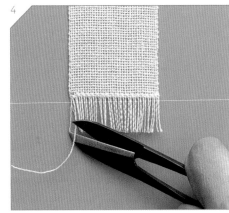

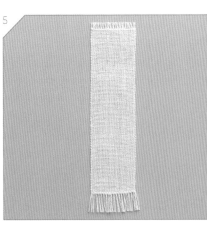

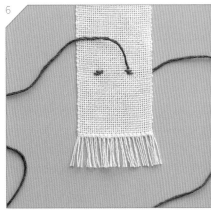

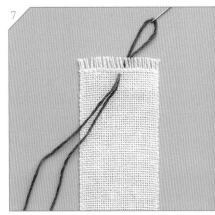

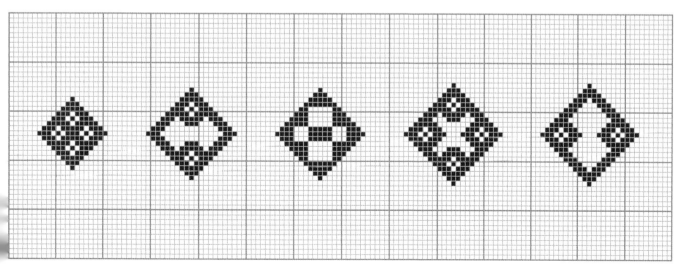

From left to right—*Kogin patterns #4, #6, #5, #8, and #7 (p. 98)*

Coasters

you use cloth made specially for kogin,
ou will get a tall diamond shape. The
ombination of dark-blue cloth and light-
ay thread gives it a very traditional feel.
or these pieces, I used split woolen yarn
stead of embroidery floss.

nished size
x 4¾ in. (12 x 12 cm)

terials for each coaster
x 4¾ in. (12 x 12 cm) of Daruma kogin cloth
(navy blue)
yd. (114 cm) of woolen yarn (light gray)
ving thread to match the fabric

Right: *Kogin pattern #13* Mameko no yotsukogori

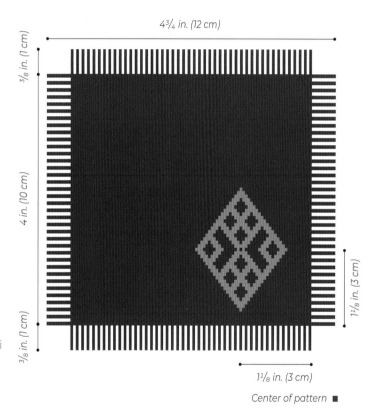

4¾ in. (12 cm)

⅜ in. (1 cm)

4 in. (10 cm)

⅜ in. (1 cm)

1⅛ in. (3 cm)

1⅛ in. (3 cm)

Center of pattern ■

1. Prepare a 4¾ in. (12 cm) square piece of cloth.

2. Pull a thread out of the weave ⅜ in. (1 cm) from each side, where you want the finished edge to be.

3. After the weave threads on, all four sides are pulled out.

4. Hem with a thread of matching color.

5. When all four sides are hemmed, pull out the rest of the weave around the outside.

6. Begin stitching near the center of the pattern (in the corner of the fabric, 1⅛ in. [3 cm] up from the bottom and in from the right).

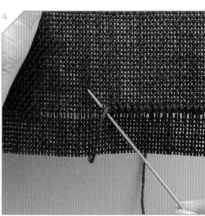

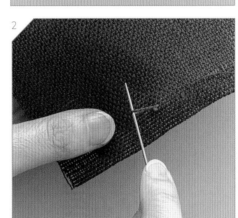

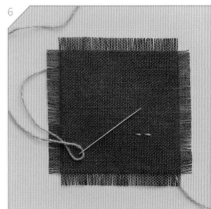

Tip: How to sew a hem

Insert the needle where you have removed one thread. Bring it back out two threads over, so that it crosses two threads diagonally on the backside. Repeat.

Tip: When using woolen yarn

If the yarn is too thick, separate the strands and adjust to your preferred thickness.

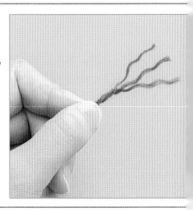

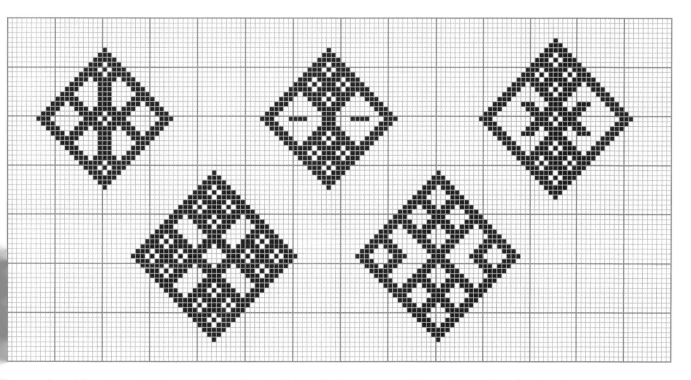

Top row, from left to right—*Kogin patterns #9, #10, and #11 (p. 98); below—arranged from #18 (p. 100), and #13 (p. 99)*

Pincushions

small hishizashi pattern is embroidered
n an old-fashioned pincushion. The
side is stuffed with raw wool. The
nolin in raw wool prevents needles
om rusting.

nished size
x 2½ in. (6.3 x 6.3 cm), 1⅛ in. (2.8 cm) thick

aterials for each pin cushion
x 4¾ in. (21 x 12 cm) of Zweigart Cashel (Amsterdam
blue), 28 count
d. (1.8 m) of sashiko thread
(beige, dark blue, greenish blue)
ndful (0.2 oz. / 5 g) of wool for stuffing
wing thread to match the fabric

Right: *Hishizashi pattern #44* Yabane

Center of pattern ▪
Finished size ▨

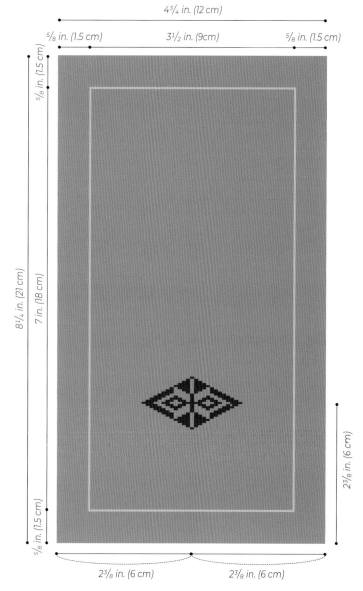

1. Prepare a piece of cloth 4¾ x 8¼ in. (12 x 21 cm).

2. Stitch the pattern with the center 2⅜ in. (6 cm) from the bottom.

3. Fold the cloth in half with the inside out and sew it together ⅝ in. (1.5 cm) from the edges, leaving a 1½ in. (4 cm) opening to turn it out.

4. Pull the needle off the remaining thread without cutting it. Turn the cloth right side out.

5. Pull the loose end of thread to the outside with a needle.

6. Stuff it with batting.

7. Thread the needle with the thread you pulled out in step 5, and sew up the opening.

8. Fold the corners inward and tie them together with doubled-up thread.

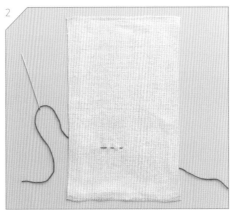

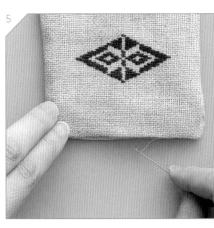

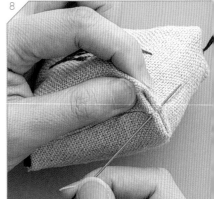

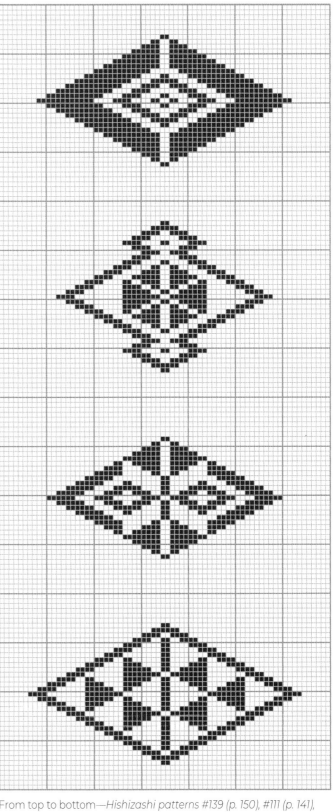

From top to bottom—*Hishizashi patterns #139 (p. 150), #111 (p. 141), #44 (p. 125), and #56 (p. 127)*

Sachets

hese simple hishizashi patterns have a
efined look with the white-and-light-
ray color scheme. A little work makes
pecial bags to wrap up your favorite
cents.

nished size
 2¼ in. (7.5 x 6 cm)

aterials for each sachet
 3½ in. (20 x 9 cm) of Zweigart Cashel (ivory) for outer,
   28 count
 x 3⅛ in. (16 x 8 cm) of thin cotton fabric for lining
d. (90 cm) of sashiko thread
   (light purple)
½ in. (80 cm) of string, 1/16 in. (1.5 mm) thick
wing thread to match the fabric

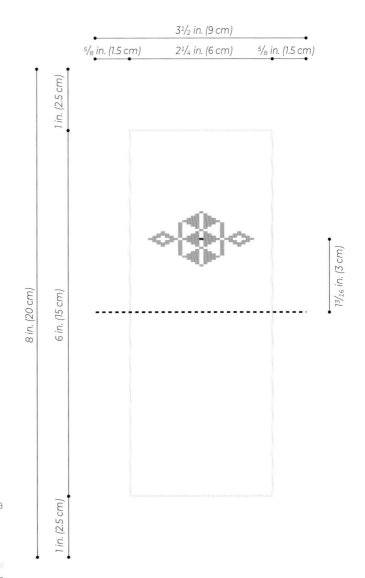

Right: *Hishizashi pattern #25* Sorobandama

Center of pattern ■
Finished size ▨
Fold line ▬ ▬

1. Prepare a piece of cloth 3½ x 8 in. (9 x 20 cm).

2. Stitch the pattern with the center 1³/₁₆ in. (3 cm) above the center of the fabric.

3. Fold the cloth in half with the inside out and sew together 2⅜ in. (6 cm) of the left and right sides, ⅝ in. (1.5 cm) from the edges.

4. Turn the cloth right side out. Fold the mouth of the bag down inside it, so that it is 3 in. (7.5 cm) tall.

5. Fold the inner cloth in half and sew up both sides, ⅜ in. (1 cm) in from the edges.

6. Fold the edge flaps back, then fold the mouth of the bag down on the outside, so that it is 2½ in. (6.5 cm) tall, making sure to keep the edges flat.

7. Put the inner bag into the outer and sew them together.

8. Pass two strings through the loops from opposite sides and tie the ends.

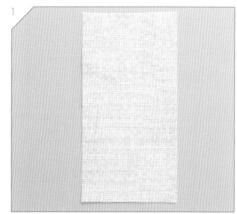

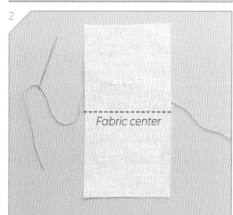

Fabric center

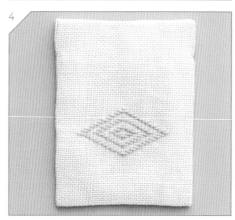

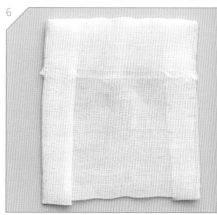

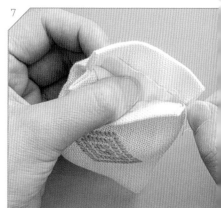

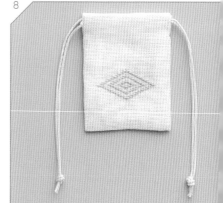

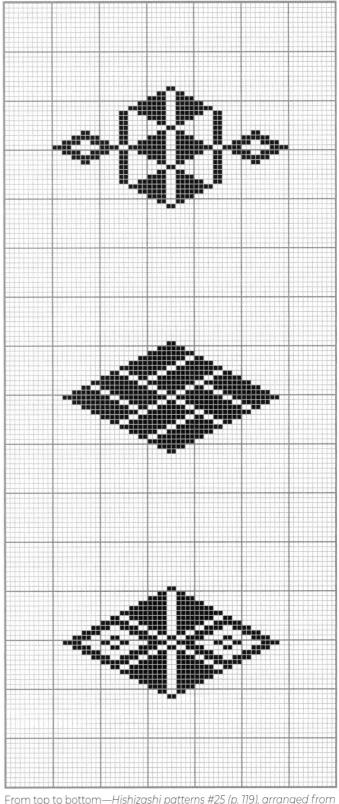

From top to bottom—*Hishizashi patterns #25 (p. 119), arranged from #120 (p.143), and #71 (p. 131)*

Cover Cloth

This is a cover cloth with many uses. In the center of the plain white cloth, there is a continuous hishizashi pattern in bright blue. The hem is tailored using the *origuke* stitch, a kimono-sewing technique.

Finished size
14½ x 14½ in. (37 x 37 cm)

Materials
16½ x 16½ in. (42 x 42 cm) of even-weave cotton fabric (ivory), 25 count
15 yd. (14 m) of Daruma kogin thread (ruri blue #6)
Sewing thread to match the fabric

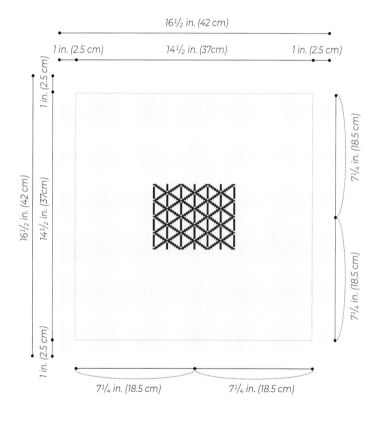

Center of pattern ■
Finished size ▨

How to fold the corners of a cloth like a picture frame by using *origuke.*

Origuke is a hand-sewing technique in which the needle is passed through a folded edge so that the stitching is almost invisible. I have used a contrasting color in the photos so that it is easy to see. Normally a thread of the same color as the cloth is used.

1a. Draw the finished size on the cloth, leaving 1 in. (2.5 cm) extra around the edges.

1b. Fold the edge of the fabric in to the line.

2a. Fold again with the same width as 1b.

2b. Fold the corner up to the line.

3. Fold the bottom edge of the fabric up to the line.

4. Fold again with the same width as step 3 and crease.

5. Unfold step 4. Then, going in through the end of the long flap, bring the needle out through the folded edge of the corner.

6. Refold step 4. Moving the needle inside the folded corner, make three diagonal stitches. Make the stitches as small as you can. These stitches are about $1/32$–$1/16$ in. (1–2 mm).

7. Put the next stitch in the edge of the right-hand fold, to connect the two flaps.

8. Sew the flap down by its edge, as shown in the picture (*origuke*).

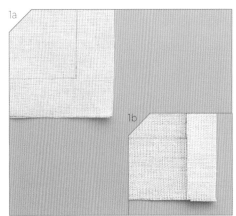

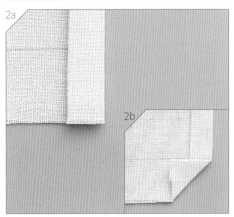

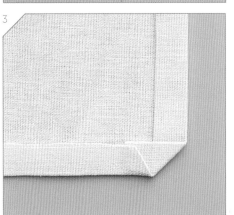

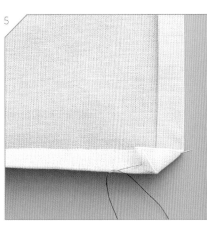

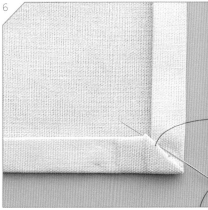

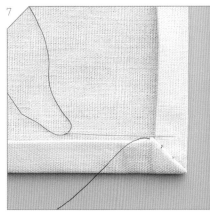

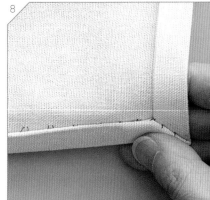

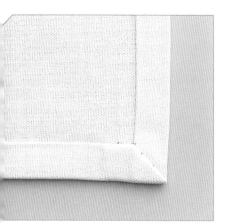

Pull the thread tight to finish. All four corners are sewn in the same way, and the sashiko pattern goes in the center of the fabric.

Final embroidered piece

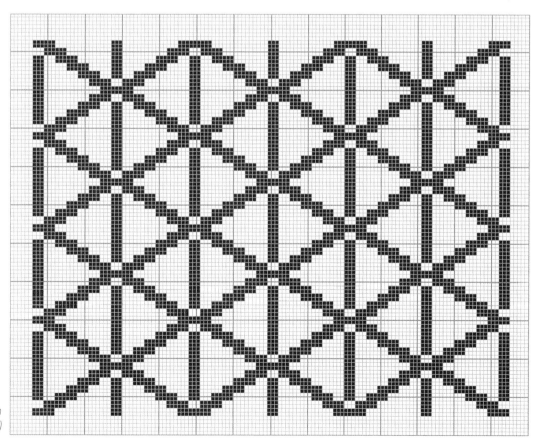

shizashi pattern arranged from #184 (p. 162)

Brooches

you choose a dense continuous pattern
will stand out, even in a small area. The
olor of the thread and the way you cut
ut the pattern will totally change the
ok, so don't be afraid to try it in various
ays and colors.

iished size
ge: 1½ x 1½ in. (3.8 x 3.8 cm)
all: 1¼ x 1¼ in. (3.3 x 3.3 cm)

terials for each brooch
3 in. (7.6 x 7.6 cm) of Zweigert Cashel (raw linen), 28
count
d. (2.7 m) of sashiko thread
(blue, dark blue, dark gray, gray, red)
-cover brooch kit

Right: *Hishizashi pattern*
#175 Ami no fushi–net knots

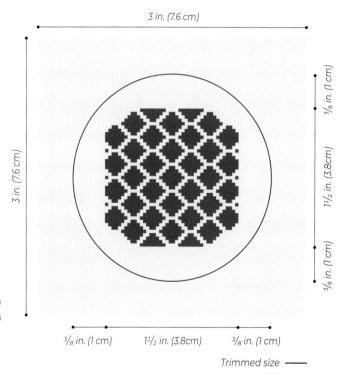

3 in. (7.6 cm)

3 in. (7.6 cm)

³⁄₈ in. (1 cm)

1½ in. (3.8cm)

³⁄₈ in. (1 cm)

³⁄₈ in. (1 cm)   1½ in. (3.8cm)   ³⁄₈ in. (1 cm)

Trimmed size ——

1. Prepare a cloth 3 in. (7.6 cm) square. Using cardboard or something similar as a template, draw a circle a little larger than the button core you want to use.

2. Stitch the pattern (this one is *hishizashi pattern #176* Fune no ho–ship's sail) so that it fills the circle you drew in step 1.

3. Cut the cloth into a round shape with about ⅜ in. (1 cm) extra around the edge of the pattern for sewing.

4. Sew around the outside, so that the ends come out on the front.

5. Put the button core on the backside and pull both ends of the thread you sewed in step 4.

6. Pull the ends tight and tie them off.

7. Apply glue to the brooch base.

8. Stick the button to the brooch base and you are finished.

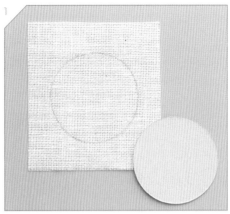

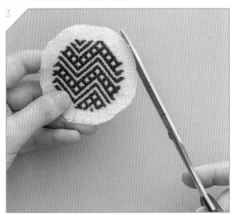

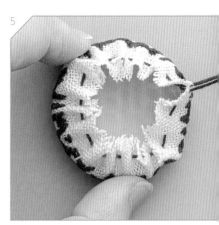

you have no brooch base

Cut some felt a little smaller than the button and sew a brooch pin to it.

Apply glue to the felt and glue it on at stage 6.

Top row, from left to right—*Kogin pattern #30 (p. 102); Hishizashi patterns #195 (p. 165), and arranged from #179 (p. 160); below—Kogin pattern #37 (p. 103), and Hishizashi pattern #175 (p. 159)*

Ribbon Hatband

...made a detachable hatband by using ...continuous kogin pattern. It would be ...n to match various hatbands to ...ur different outfits.

...nished size
...dth: 2 in. (5 cm)
...ngth: depends on size of the hat

...aterials
...½–35½ in. (80–90 cm) of Vaupel & Heilenbeck linen band ...(raw linen), 4 in. (10 cm) wide, 20 count
...yd. (24 m) of kogin thread (gray)
...wing thread to match the fabric

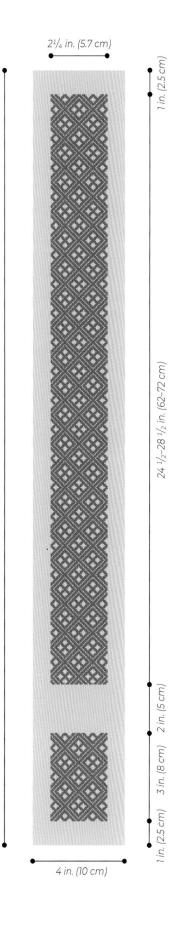

2¼ in. (5.7 cm)

1 in. (2.5 cm)

31½–35½ in. (80–90 cm)

24 ½–28 ½ in. (62–72 cm)

2 in. (5 cm)

3 in. (8 cm)

1 in. (2.5 cm)

4 in. (10 cm)

1. Stitch the pattern on a 4 in. (10 cm) wide strip of linen tape.

2. The finished embroidery, with a separate section for covering the knot.

3. Cut off the piece that will cover the knot.

4. Fold the edges together in the back and hem them together, making sure that they do not overlap (both pieces).

5. Tuck one end into the other end, pinch the edges together, and sew them in place.

6. Wrap the small piece around the main piece, covering the seam from step 5. Sew closed at the back.

7. Ready to put on your hat.

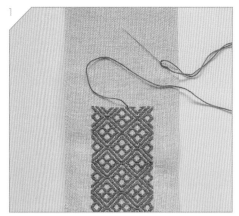

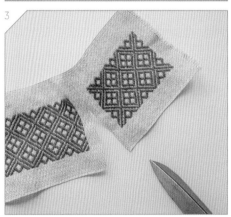

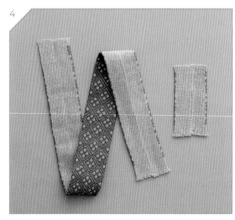

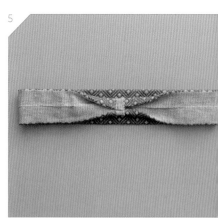

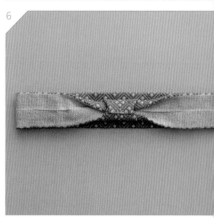

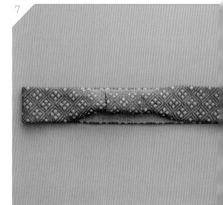

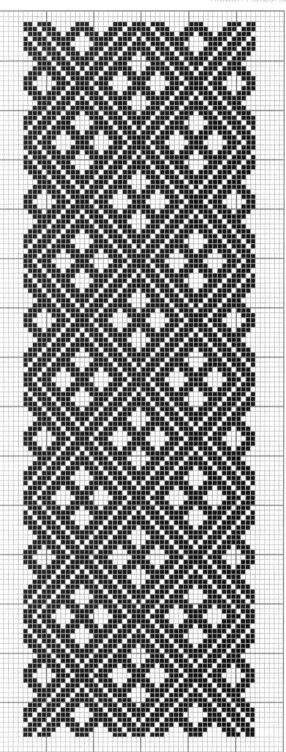

Kogin pattern arranged from #3 (p. 98) and #38 (p. 104)

Tote Bag

classic mini tote with continuous
ishizashi patterns in black thread. The
arying density of several patterns makes
his design different and interesting.

nished size
¼ x 9½ in. (26 x 24 cm) excluding handles

aterials
x 11 in. (58 x 28 cm) of Zweigart Cashel (raw linen) for
outer, 28 count
x 11 in. (58 x 28 cm) of cotton fabric for lining
yd. (90 m) of sashiko thread (black)
⁄2 x 9½ in. (34 x 24 cm) of cotton fabric for handles (black)
wing thread to match the fabric

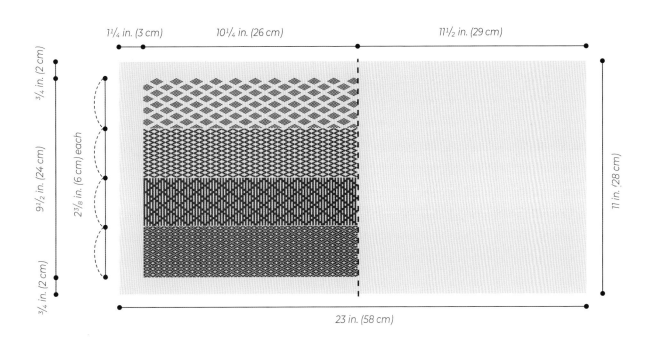

1¼ in. (3 cm) 10¼ in. (26 cm) 11½ in. (29 cm)

¾ in. (2 cm)
9½ in. (24 cm)
2³⁄8 in. (6 cm) each
¾ in. (2 cm)
11 in. (28 cm)

23 in. (58 cm)

Making Handles

1a. Fold the cloth in the center and crease it (crease line a).

1b. Fold both sides of the cloth into the center crease.

1c. Fold once more at the center line to make a strip a quarter the original width.

1d. Sew the edges together.

2. Stitch the pattern according to the diagram.

3. The finished embroidery

4. Fold fabric in half with the front of the embroidery on the inside and sew both sides together ¾ in. (2 cm) from the edge. Sew the lining in the same way.

Note: Since embroidery can cause shrinkage of the outer cloth, adjust the size of the lining to match at this point.

5. Iron both the outer and lining with the seams folded to one side. Turn the outer to the right side and press.

6. Place the lining inside the outer. When doing so, fold the seams to alternate sides.

7. Fold the excess on the mouth of the bag (both outer and lining) to the inside and insert the handles in between the two pieces. Sew the outer and lining together at the mouth of the bag.

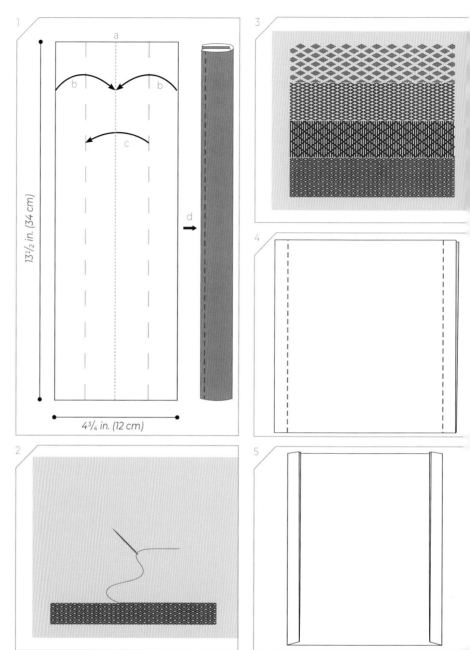

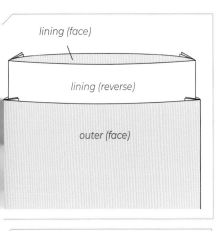

lining (face)

lining (reverse)

outer (face)

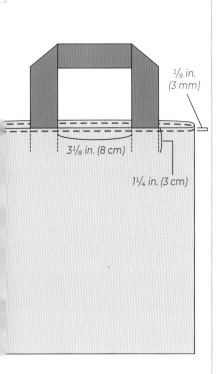

¹⁄₈ in.
(3 mm)

3¹⁄₈ in. (8 cm)

1¹⁄₄ in. (3 cm)

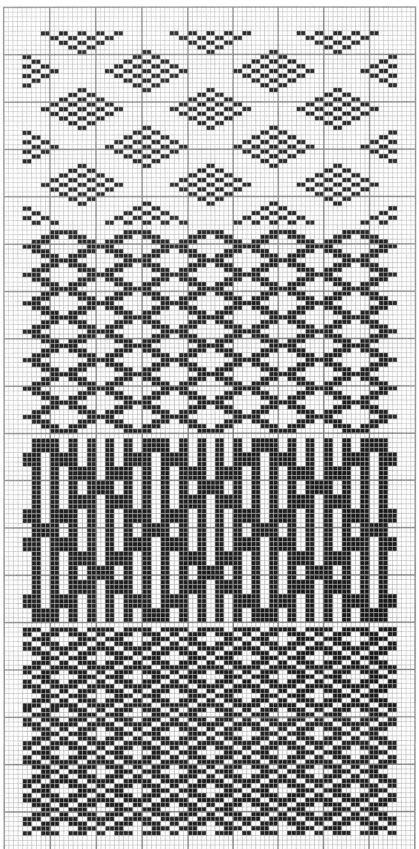

top to bottom—*Hishizashi patterns #194 (p. 165), #181
(p. 161), #178 (p. 160), and #183 (p. 162)*

Cushion Covers

is also nice to combine your favorite
atterns and arrange them in one
rge diamond. These cushions are
mbroidered with thick woolen yarn
 match the wool fabric. Counted
ashiko embroidery can be done on
ny fabric, so long as it is plain weave
nd the threads can be counted.

nished size
x 17 in. (43 x 43 cm)

aterials for each cover
x 19 in. (48 x 48 cm) of even-weave woolen fabric for the
   front, 11 count
x 26 in. (48 x 66 cm) of cotton fabric for the back
yd. (20 m) of woolen yarn
   (gray, ivory)
n. (43 cm) square cushion pad
wing thread to match the fabric

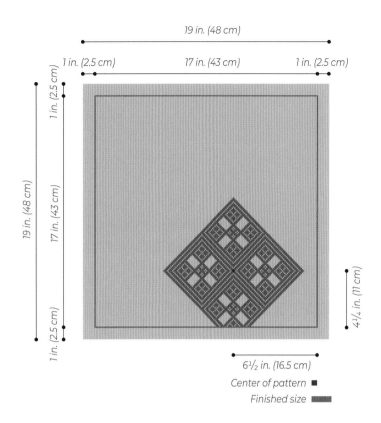

19 in. (48 cm)

1 in. (2.5 cm) 17 in. (43 cm) 1 in. (2.5 cm)

1 in. (2.5 cm)

19 in. (48 cm)

17 in. (43 cm)

1 in. (2.5 cm)

1 in. (2.5 cm)

4¼ in. (11 cm)

6½ in. (16.5 cm)

Center of pattern ■
Finished size ▬

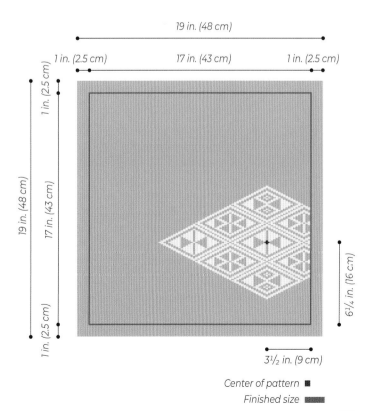

19 in. (48 cm)

1 in. (2.5 cm) 17 in. (43 cm) 1 in. (2.5 cm)

1 in. (2.5 cm)

19 in. (48 cm)

17 in. (43 cm)

1 in. (2.5 cm)

1 in. (2.5 cm)

6¼ in. (16 c.m)

3½ in. (9 cm)

Center of pattern ■
Finished size ▬

1. Stitch the pattern according to the diagram.

2. After the embroidery is finished, sew the front and back pieces together as in the illustration, folding the seams toward the center. Fold both ends over twice and sew them.

3. Fold so that the ends overlap by 3½ in. (9 cm) and sew the top and bottom.

4. Turn it right side out, iron, and insert the cushion.

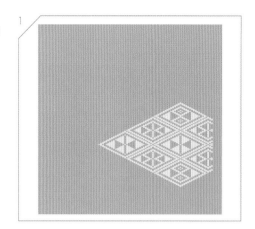

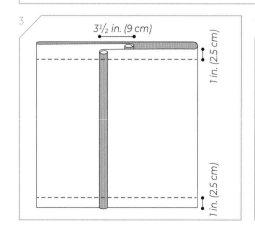

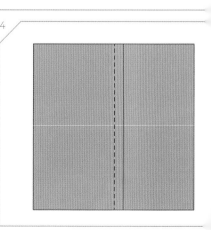

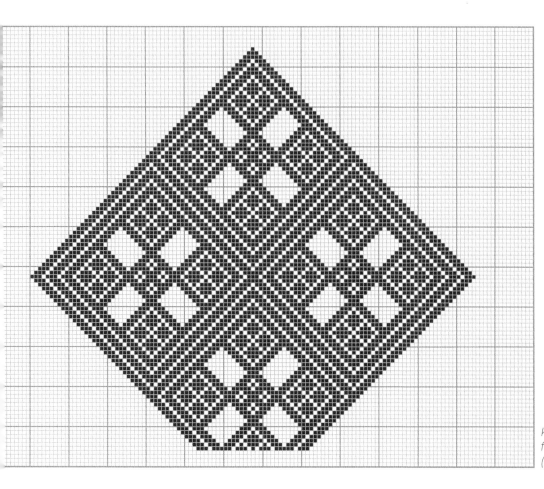

Kogin patterns arranged from #4 (p.98) and #19 (p. 100), and #38 (p. 104)

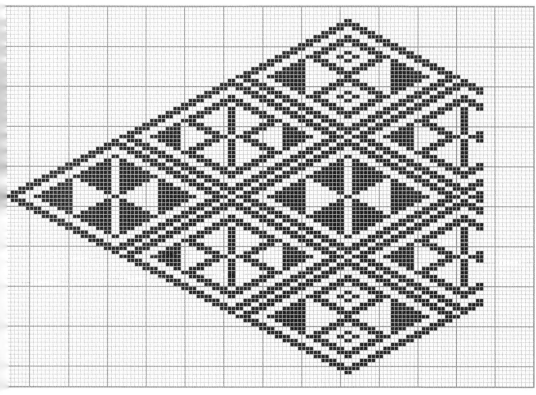

Hishizashi patterns #22 (p. 119), #55 (p. 127), and #151 (p. 153)

abric Panel

olors inspired by medieval kimonos
e arranged in a continuous hishizashi
ittern. You could put it in a frame and
ijoy it as a small art piece.

ished size

6¼ in. (15 x 16 cm)

terials

8¼ in. (20 x 21 cm) of Zweigart Cashel (light mocha)
for the front, 28 count

8¼ in. (20 x 21 cm) of cotton fabric for the back

d. (23 m) of sashiko thread (cream)

d (1.8 m) of each color of sashiko thread
blue, brown, green, mustard yellow, and red)

ving thread to match the fabric

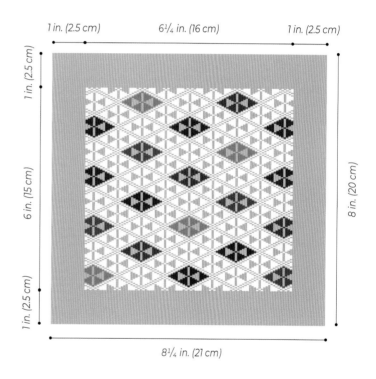

Projects

1. Start stitching with the white thread from the lower right corner.

2. Stitch up to the top edge.

3. Stitch the next column on the left.

4. Stitch the next column on the left.

5. All of the white thread portion finished

6. Stitch the colored-thread parts one pattern at a time.

7. Align the front and back cloths with their outside faces together. Sew them as shown by the dotted line, leaving a 2 in. (5 cm) opening to turn them right side out.

8. Turn it right side out, iron, and sew up the opening.

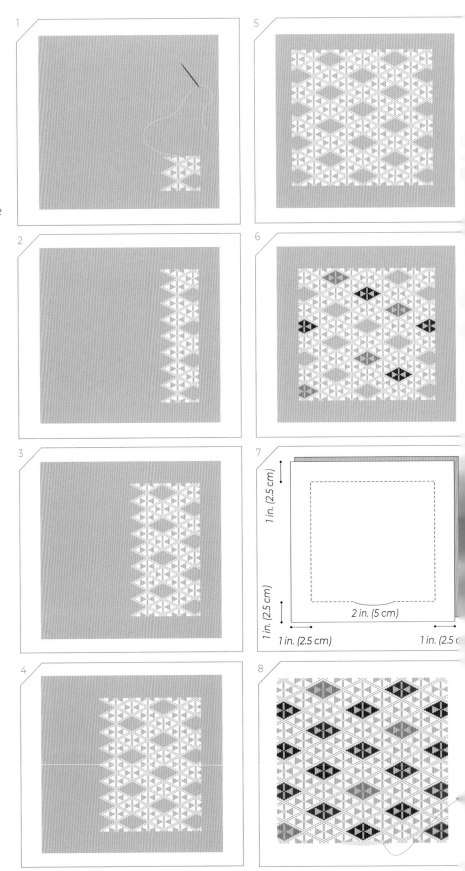

Hishizashi pattern #199 (p. 167)

Pocket

he beauty of hishizashi Maekake apron
a flat square cloth. An elaborate and
xtravagant patch pocket.

nished size
7 in. (20 x 18 cm)

aterials
x 9 in. (25 x 23 cm) of Zweigart Cashel (raw linen) for
the front, 28 count
x 9 in. (25 x 23 cm) of cotton fabric for the back
yd. (12 m) x 4 colors of sashiko thread
(deep red, gray, light beige, and navy blue)
wing thread to match the fabric

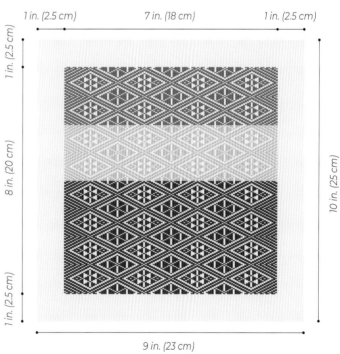

1. Just as with continuous patterns, stitch the pattern across the full width, one row at a time, changing the color periodically.

2. When the embroidery is finished, align the front and back cloths with their outside faces together. Sew them as shown by the dotted line, leaving a 2 in. (5 cm) opening to turn them right side out.

3. Turn it right side out, iron, and sew up the opening.

4. Sew it onto your pants.

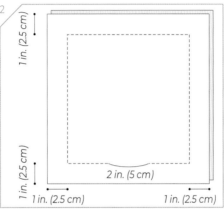

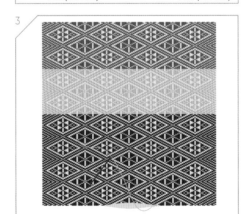

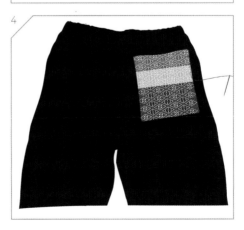

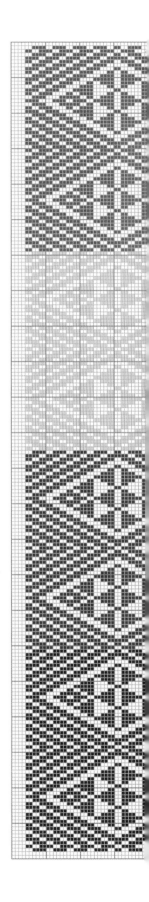

*Hishizashi patterns
#53 (p. 127), #69 (p. 131),
and #172 (p. 158)*

Tapestry

Tapestry (Kogin)

In homage to beautiful old kimonos, I reproduced their patterns and made them into a tapestry. Since it uses a special kogin fabric, the patterns come out tall like the originals.

Tapestry (Hishizashi)

I chose five patterns and arranged them into a striped design, which is one of the characteristic hishizashi designs. Traditional hishizashi aprons were often embroidered with woolen yarn, so this tapestry is done the same way.

Projects

Finished size
15¾ x 57 in. (40 x 145 cm)

Materials
19¾ x 61½ in. (50 x 156 cm) of Tsukiya Asa 252 (navy blue)
197 yd. (180 m) of Olympus kogin thread (cream #731)
Sewing thread to match the fabric

Finished size
15¾ x 57 in. (40 x 145 cm)

Materials
19¾ x 61½ in. (50 x156 cm) of Tsukiya Asa 252 (raw linen)
35 yd. (32 m) x 4 colors of Daruma wool yarn (blue, gray, ivory, and navy blue). Sewing thread to match the fabric

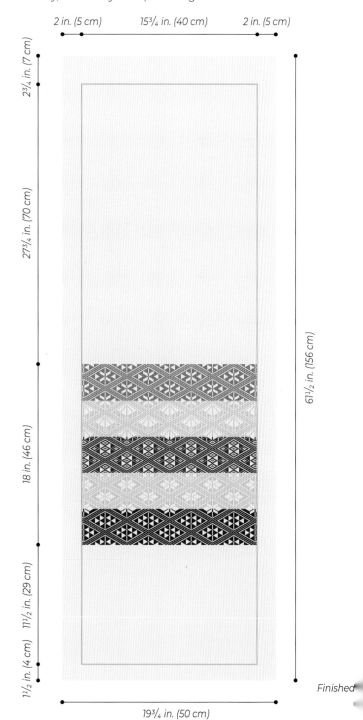

Finished

Stitch the pattern according to the diagram (quatered templates avaliable on pages 170-179). Leave a 1 in. (2.5 cm) space on both sides, bordered by a stitch spanning two warp threads. Stitch two or four rows with each piece of thread, doubling back at the end.

The back: leave all the loose ends on one side.

Stitching the bamboo border pattern at the end.

When all the embroidery is completed, cut every loose end to the same length.

The front

The back

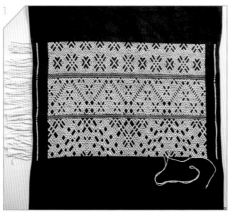

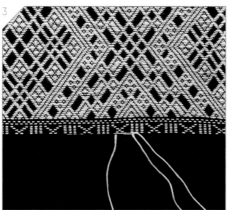

7. Fold the edge so that the border comes to the back.

8. Fold it one more time and sew with the *origuke* technique. (See pp. 62–63 for details on how to do this.)

9. Fold the bottom twice and sew the same way. Do the same with the top, but leave enough room to pass a rod through. The hishizashi piece is tailored in the same way.

   (When you actually do this, use a thread color that will not stand out.)

10. The front (before hemming)

11. The back

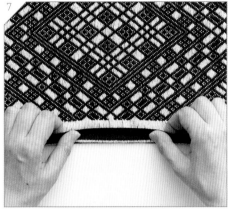

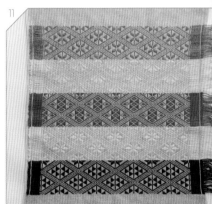

Tapestry Kogin

Kogin patterns #12 (p. 99), #55 (p. 106), #74 (p. 112), arranged from #18 (p. 100), #44 (p. 104), #22 (p. 101), #38 (p. 104), #50 (p. 105), #61 (p. 108), and #69 (p. 110)

Tapestry Hishizashi

From top to bottom—*Hishizashi patterns #48 (p. 126), #41 (p. 124),*
#5 (p. 130), #157 (p. 155), and #58 (p. 128)

The hishizashi patterns in this book are reproduced from *Nambu Tsuzu Hishizashi Moyosyu.*

TEMPLATES

Kogin Basic Patterns

基礎模様

1 *Kacharazu* (7)

2 *Hanako* (9)

3 *Mameko* (11)

4 Four *Hanako* (15)

5 *Urokogata* (19)

6 *Shimadazashi* (19)

7 *Fukube* (21)

8 *Komakurazashi* (21)

9 *Neko no ashi* (29)

10 *Neko no managu* (29)

11 *Tekonako* (33)

Kogin Basic Patterns

基
礎
模
様

12

Kinone no kikurako (35)

13

Mameko no yotsukogori (35)

14

Urokogata (37)

15

Bekozashi (37)

16

Uma no kutsuwa (39)

17

Kurubikara (39)

Kogin Basic Patterns

基礎模様

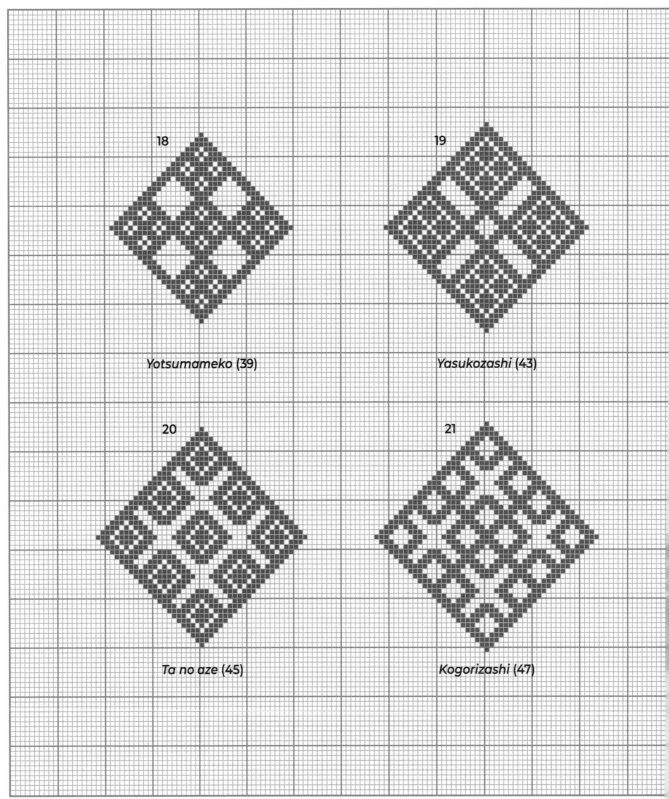

18

Yotsumameko (39)

19

Yasukozashi (43)

20

Ta no aze (45)

21

Kogorizashi (47)

Kogin Basic Patterns

基
礎
模
様

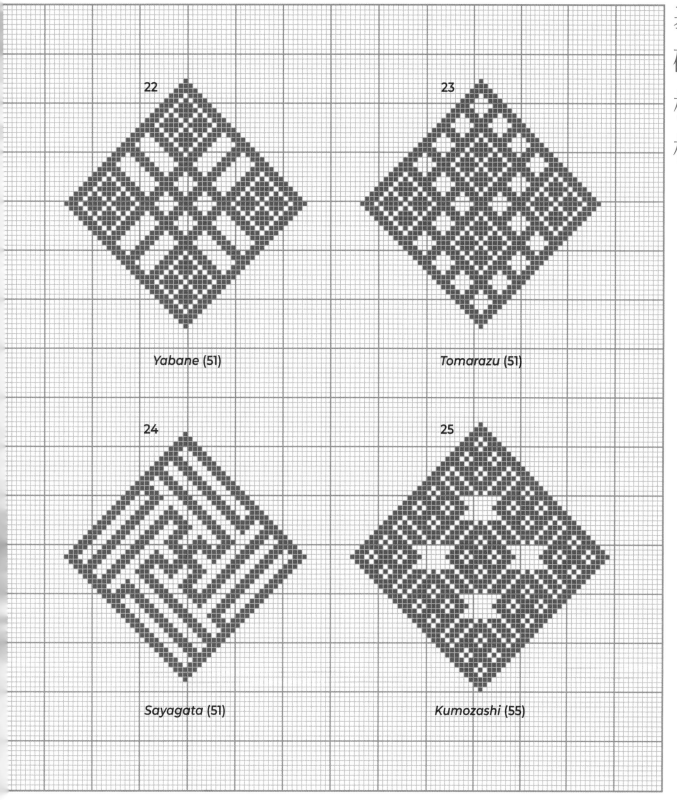

22 *Yabane* (51)

23 *Tomarazu* (51)

24 *Sayagata* (51)

25 *Kumozashi* (55)

Kogin Continuous Patterns

連続模様

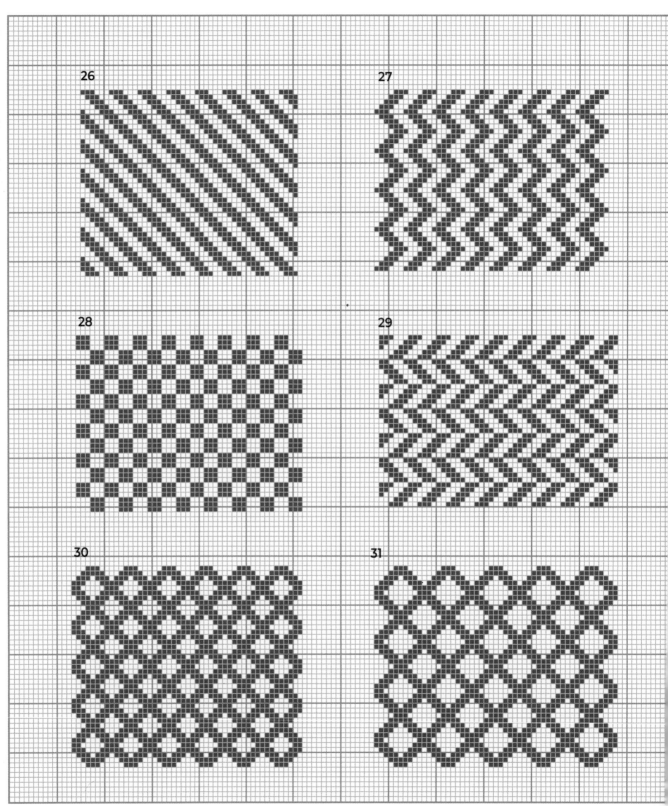

Kogin Continuous Patterns

連続模様

Kogin Diagonal Patterns

流れ・囲み模様

Kogin Diagonal Patterns

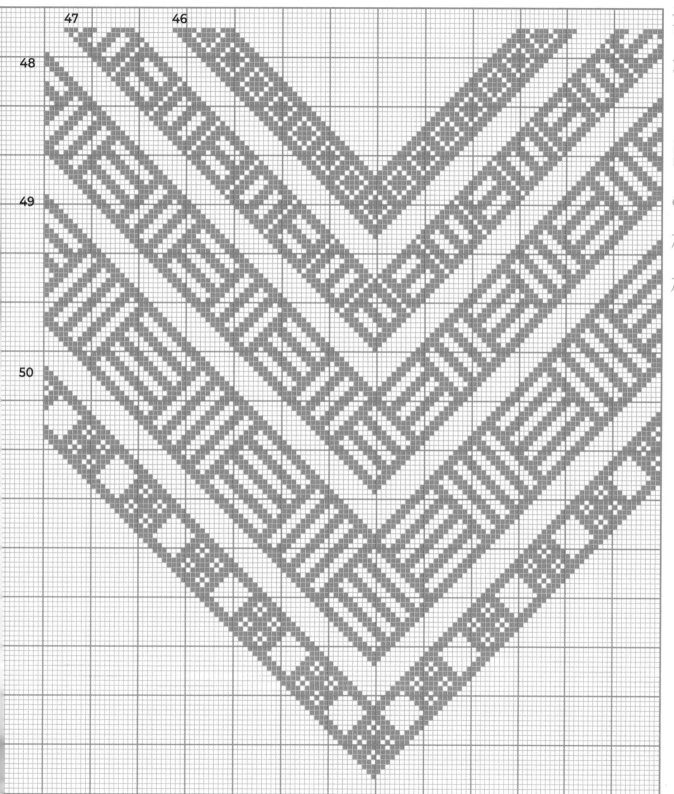

流れ・囲み模様

Kogin Diagonal Patterns

流れ・囲み模様

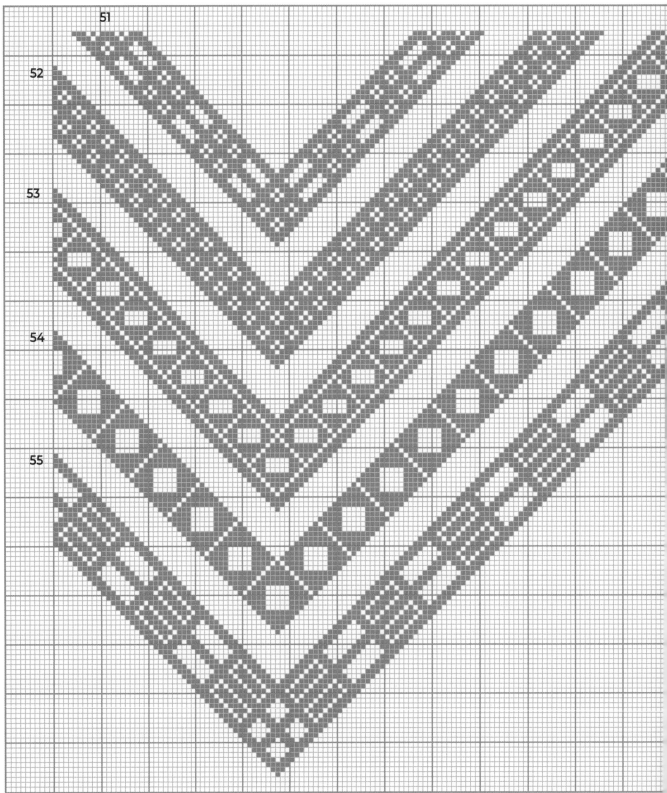

Kogin Diagonal Patterns

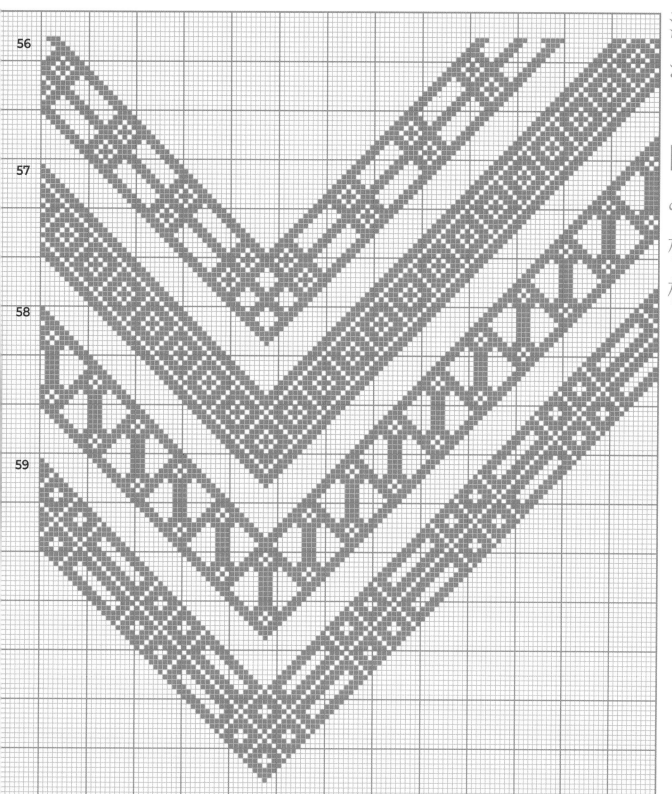

流れ・囲み模様

56

57

58

59

Kogin Diagonal Patterns

流れ・囲み模様

60

61

Kogin Diagonal Patterns

流れ・囲み模様

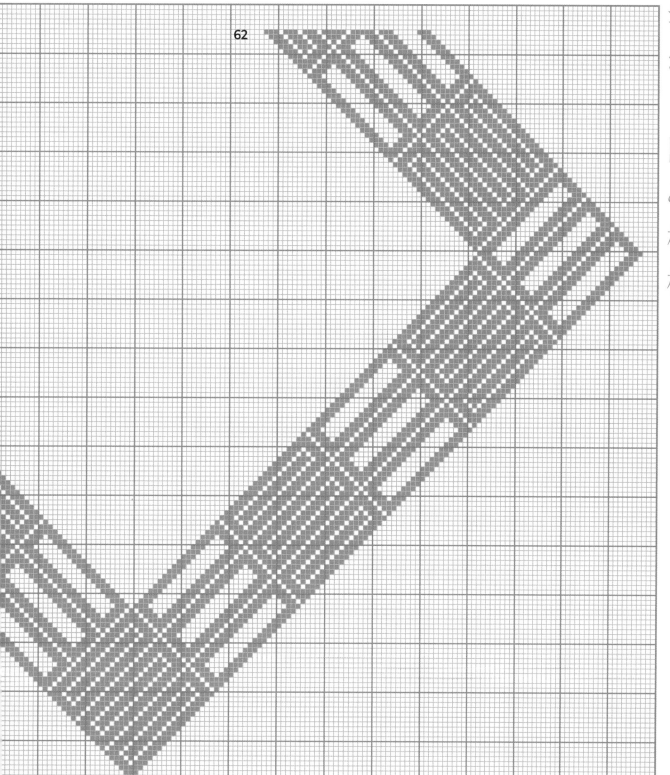

62

Kogin Bamboo Borders

竹の節

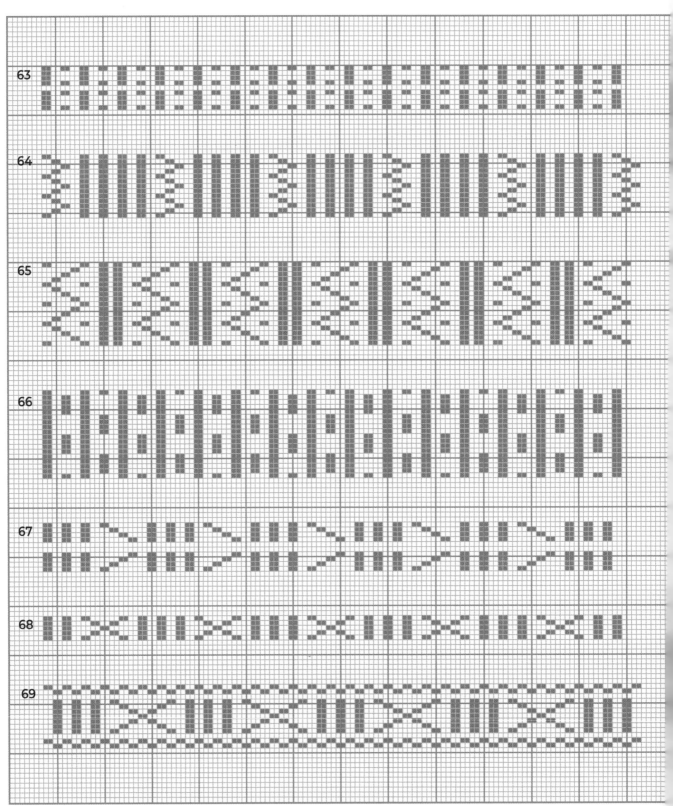

Kogin Bamboo Borders

竹
の
節

70

71

72

73

Kogin Horizontal Patterns

横模様

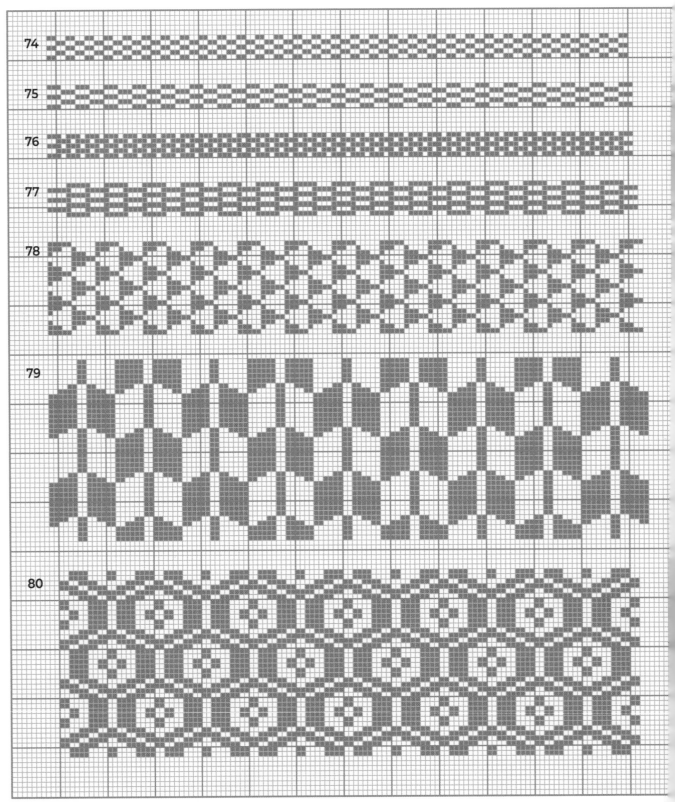

Hishizashi *Ume no hana*

梅の花

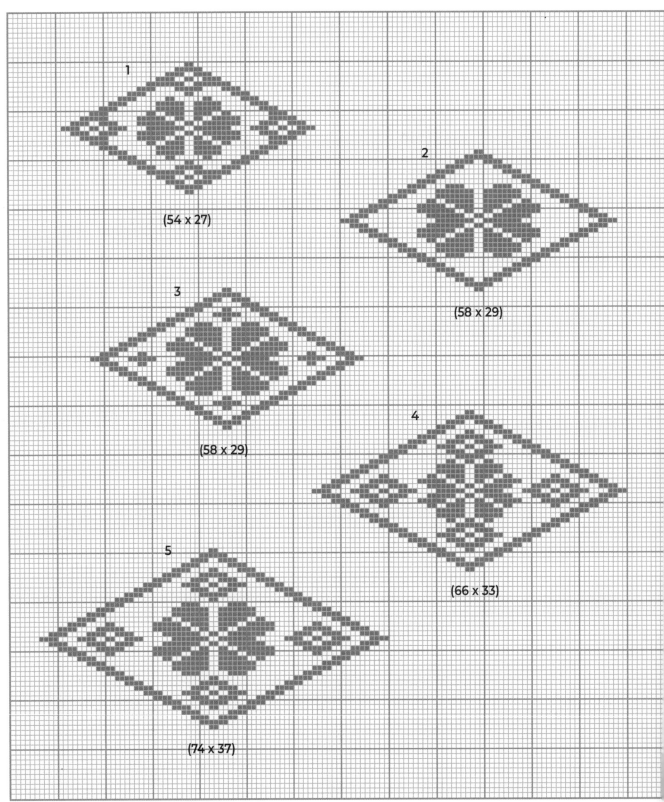

1

(54 x 27)

2

(58 x 29)

3

(58 x 29)

4

(66 x 33)

5

(74 x 37)

梅
の
花

6

(74 x 37)

7

(78 x 39)

8

(78 x 39)

Hishizashi *Beko no kura*

べこの鞍

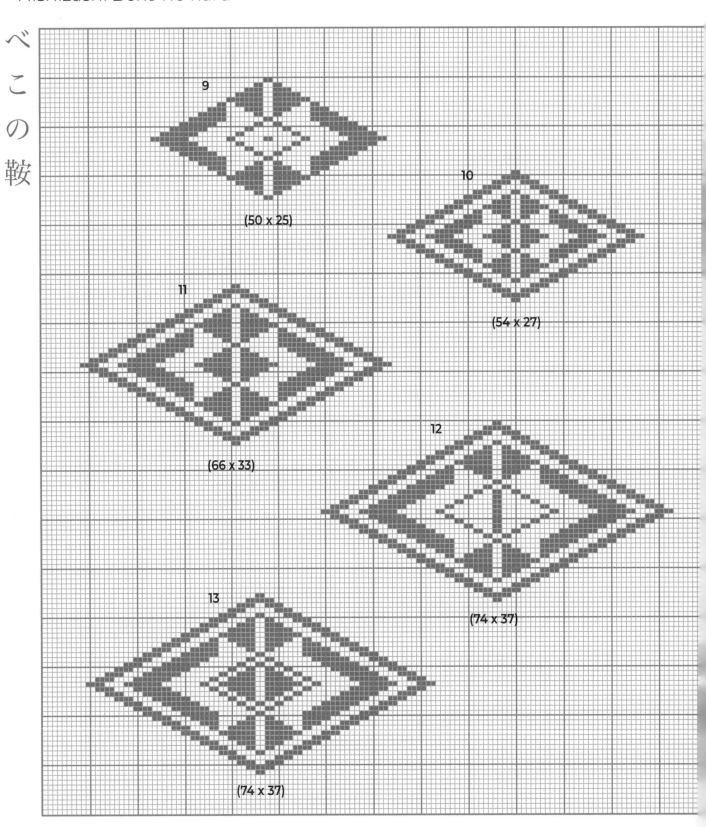

9

(50 x 25)

10

(54 x 27)

11

(66 x 33)

12

(74 x 37)

13

(74 x 37)

Hishizashi *Beko no kura*

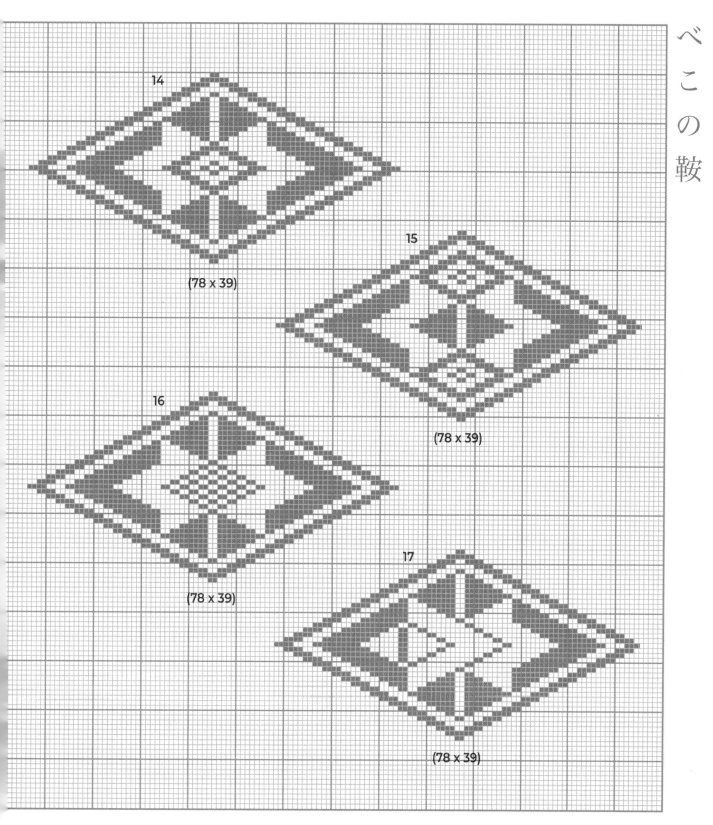

14

(78 x 39)

15

(78 x 39)

16

(78 x 39)

17

(78 x 39)

べこの鞍

Hishizashi *Beko no kura*

べこの鞍

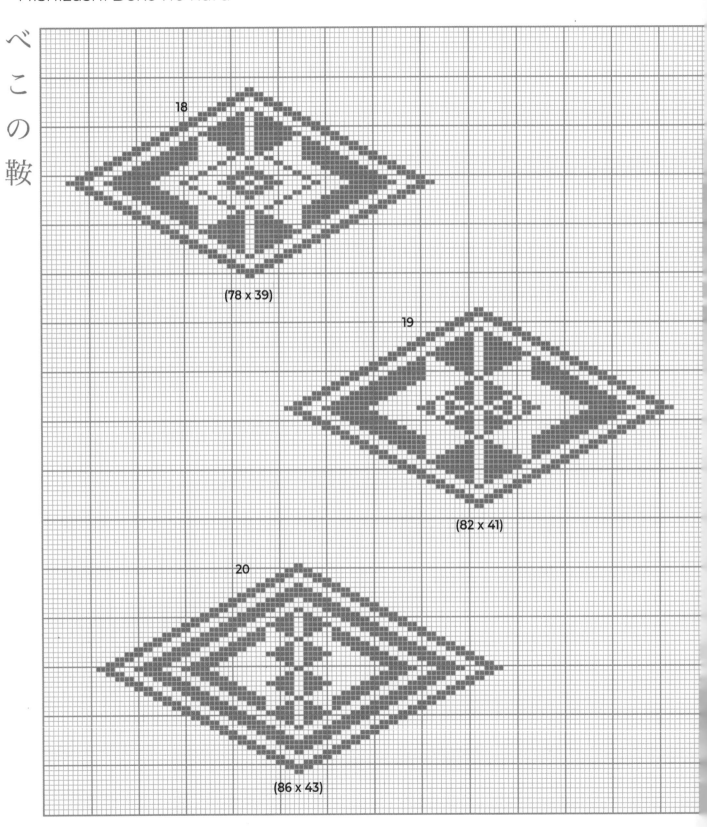

18

(78 x 39)

19

(82 x 41)

20

(86 x 43)

Hishizashi *Sorobandama*

算
盤
珠

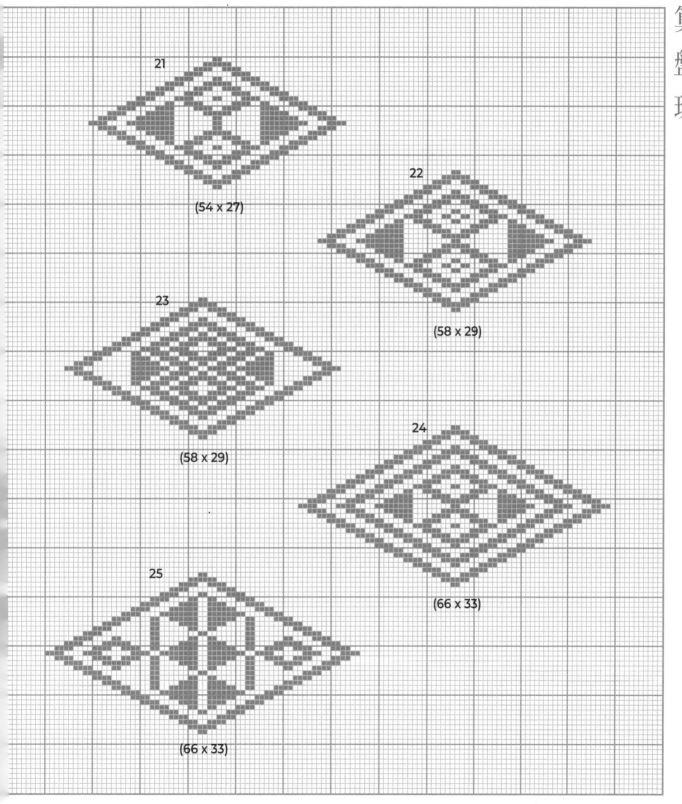

21
(54 x 27)

22
(58 x 29)

23
(58 x 29)

24
(66 x 33)

25
(66 x 33)

Hishizashi *Sorobandama*

算盤珠

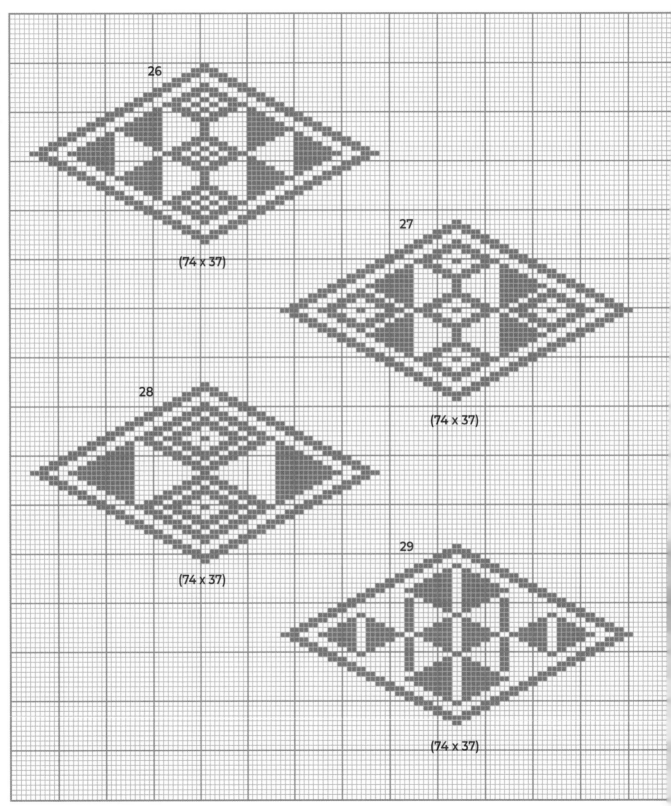

26

(74 x 37)

27

(74 x 37)

28

(74 x 37)

29

(74 x 37)

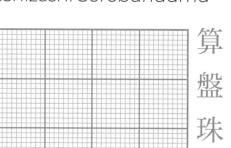

Hishizashi *Sorobandama*

算盤珠

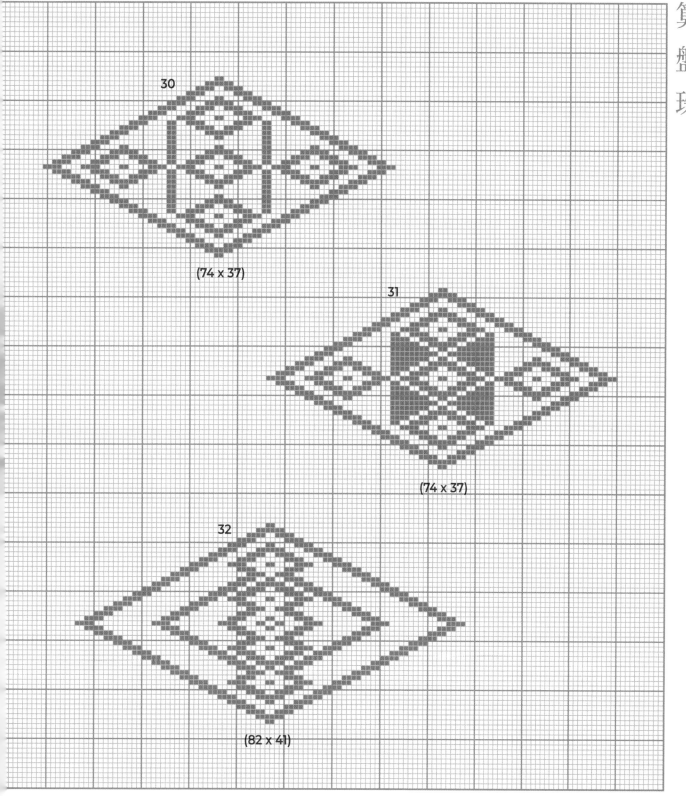

30

(74 x 37)

31

(74 x 37)

32

(82 x 41)

Hishizashi *Kiji no ashi*

雉子の足

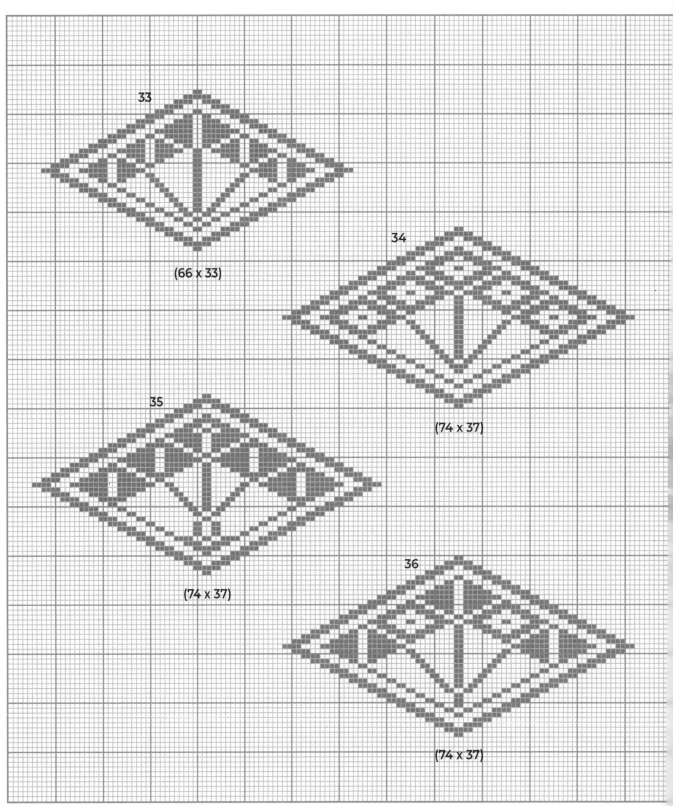

33

(66 x 33)

34

(74 x 37)

35

(74 x 37)

36

(74 x 37)

Hishizashi *Kiji no ashi*

雉
子
の
足

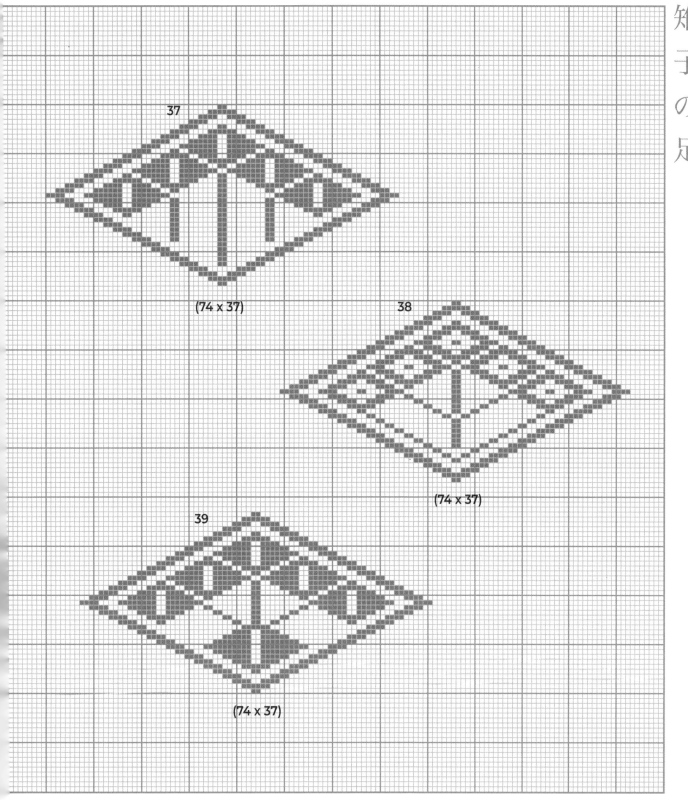

37

(74 x 37)

38

(74 x 37)

39

(74 x 37)

Hishizashi *Kiji no ashi*

雉
子
の
足

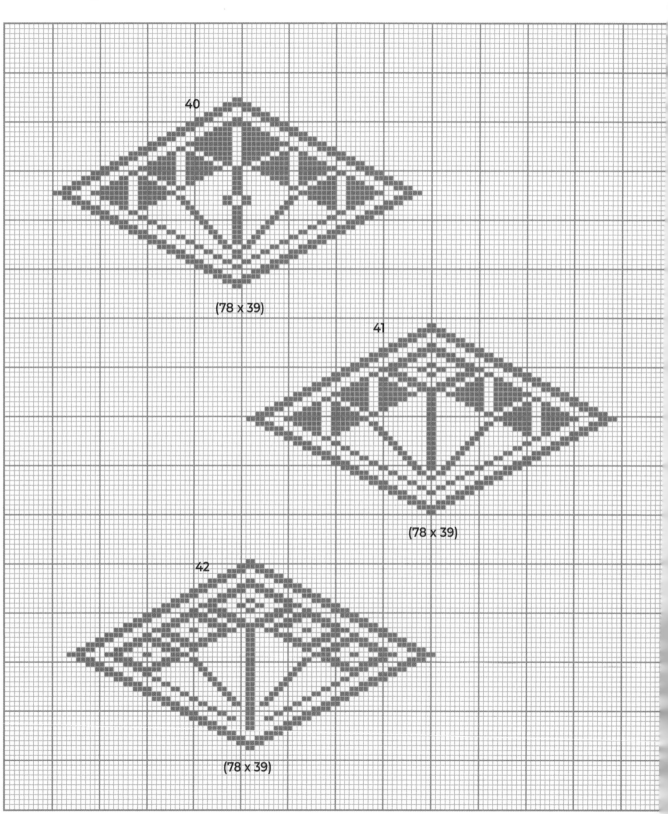

Hishizashi *Yabane*

矢羽根

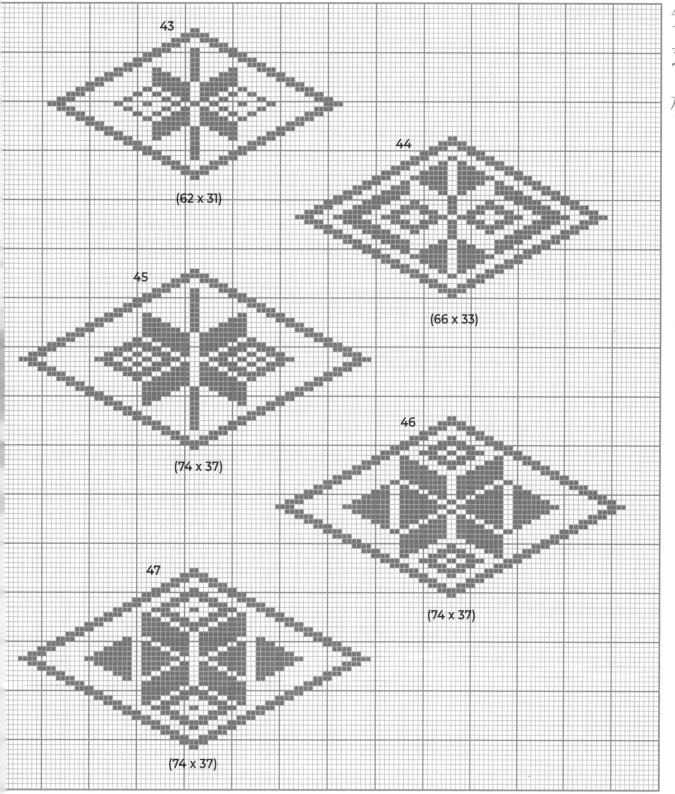

43
(62 x 31)

44
(66 x 33)

45
(74 x 37)

46
(74 x 37)

47
(74 x 37)

Hishizashi *Yabane*

矢羽根

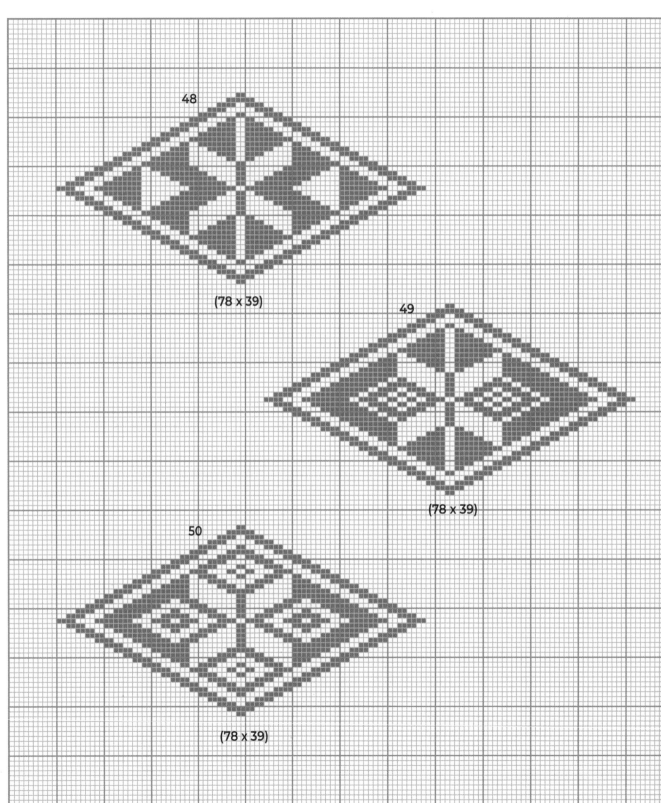

48

(78 x 39)

49

(78 x 39)

50

(78 x 39)

Hishizashi *Urokomon*

鱗
紋

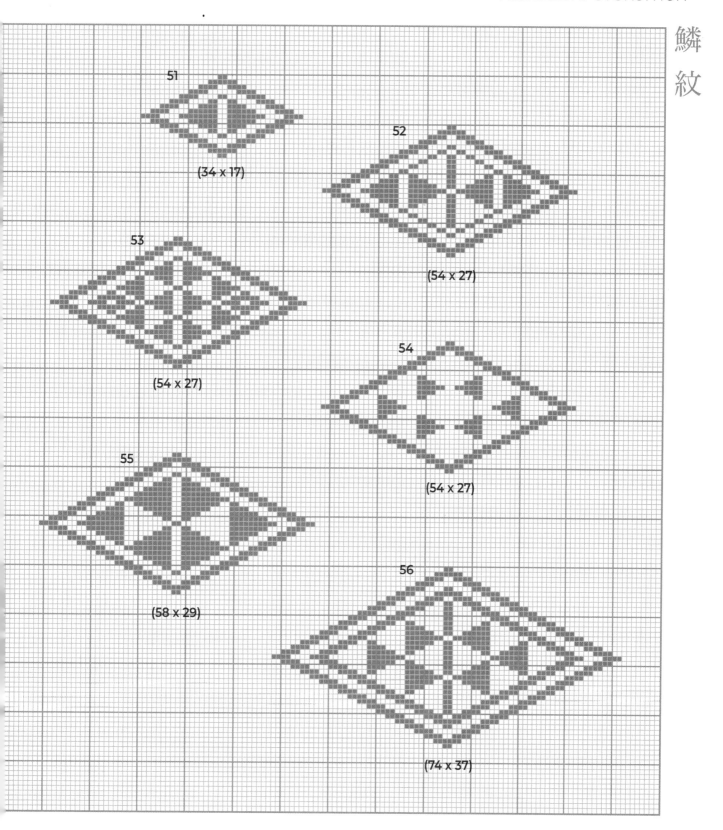

51

(34 x 17)

52

(54 x 27)

53

(54 x 27)

54

(54 x 27)

55

(58 x 29)

56

(74 x 37)

Hishizashi *Urokomon*

鱗
紋

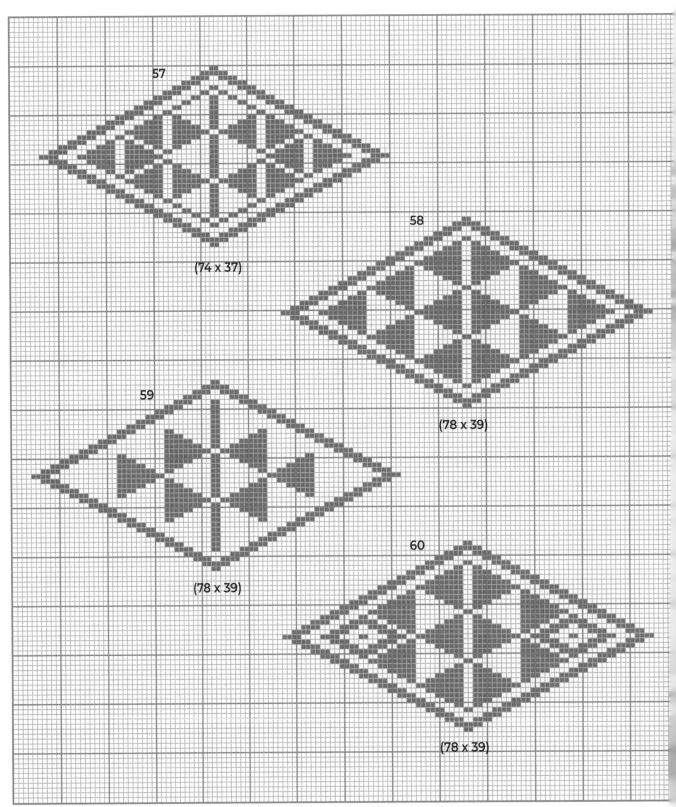

57

(74 x 37)

58

(78 x 39)

59

(78 x 39)

60

(78 x 39)

三つ菱

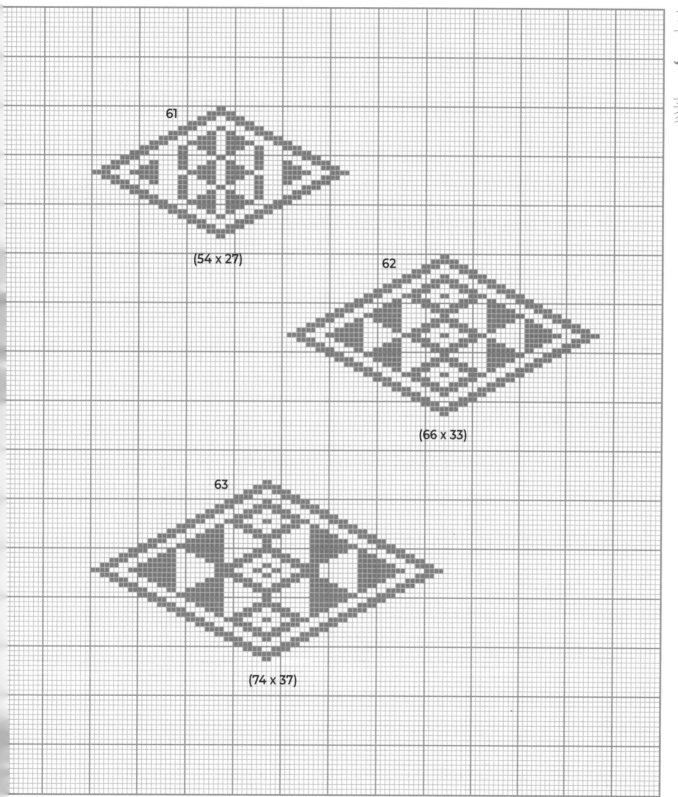

61

(54 x 27)

62

(66 x 33)

63

(74 x 37)

Hishizashi *Mitsubishi*

三つ菱

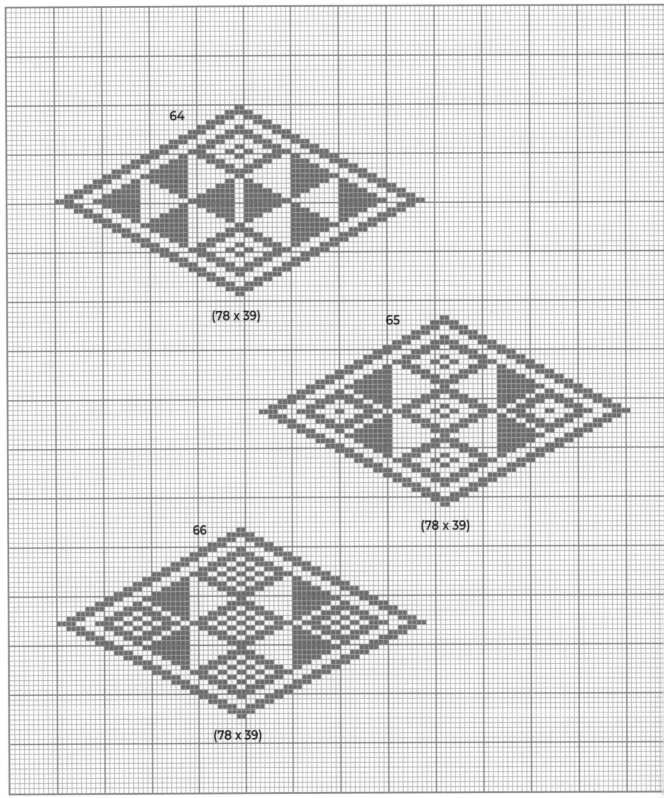

64

(78 x 39)

65

(78 x 39)

66

(78 x 39)

Hishizashi *Yotsubishi*

四つ菱

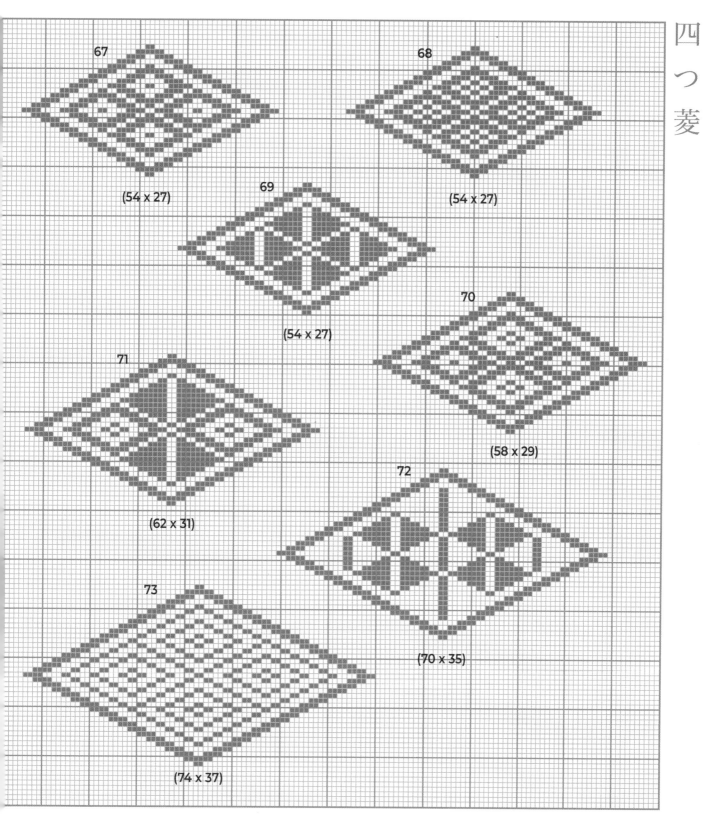

67 (54 x 27)

68 (54 x 27)

69 (54 x 27)

70 (58 x 29)

71 (62 x 31)

72 (70 x 35)

73 (74 x 37)

Hishizashi *Yotsubishi*

四つ菱

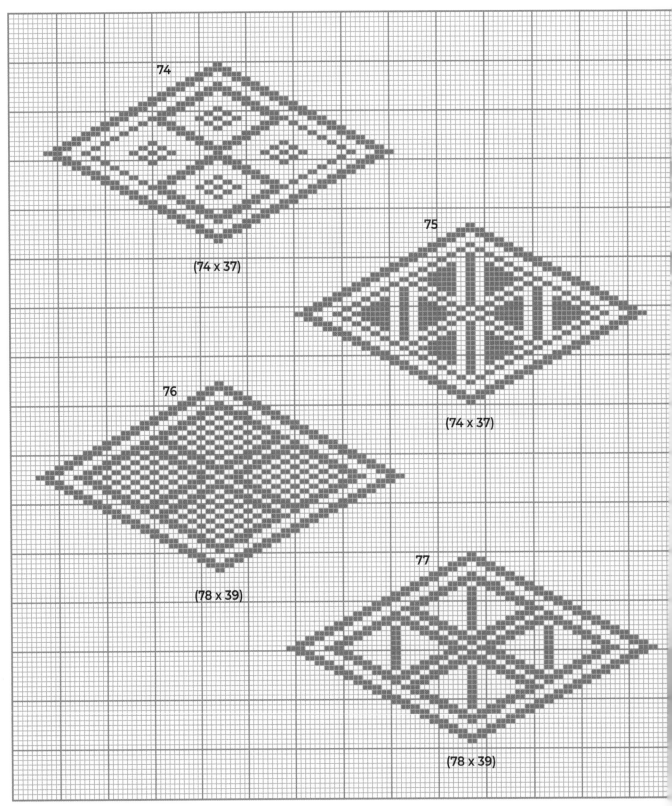

74
(74 x 37)

75
(74 x 37)

76
(78 x 39)

77
(78 x 39)

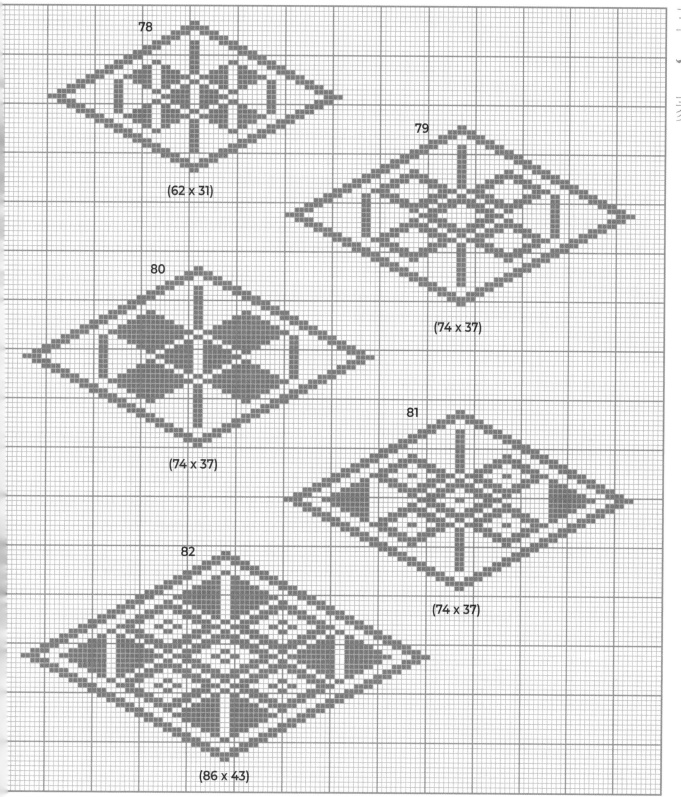
五
つ
菱

78

(62 x 31)

79

(74 x 37)

80

(74 x 37)

81

(74 x 37)

82

(86 x 43)

Hishizashi *Nanatsubishi*

七
つ
菱

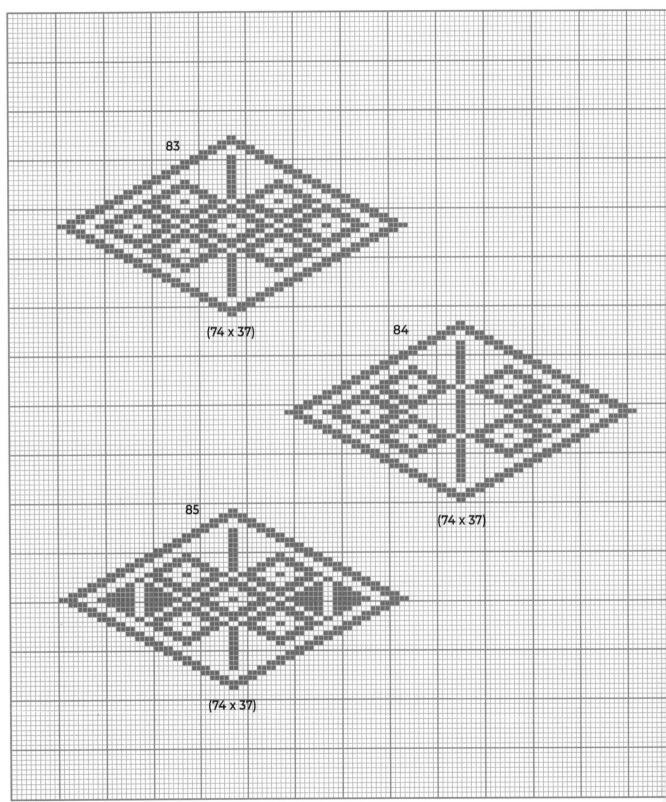

83

(74 x 37)

84

(74 x 37)

85

(74 x 37)

Hishizashi *Kokonotsubishi*

九つ菱

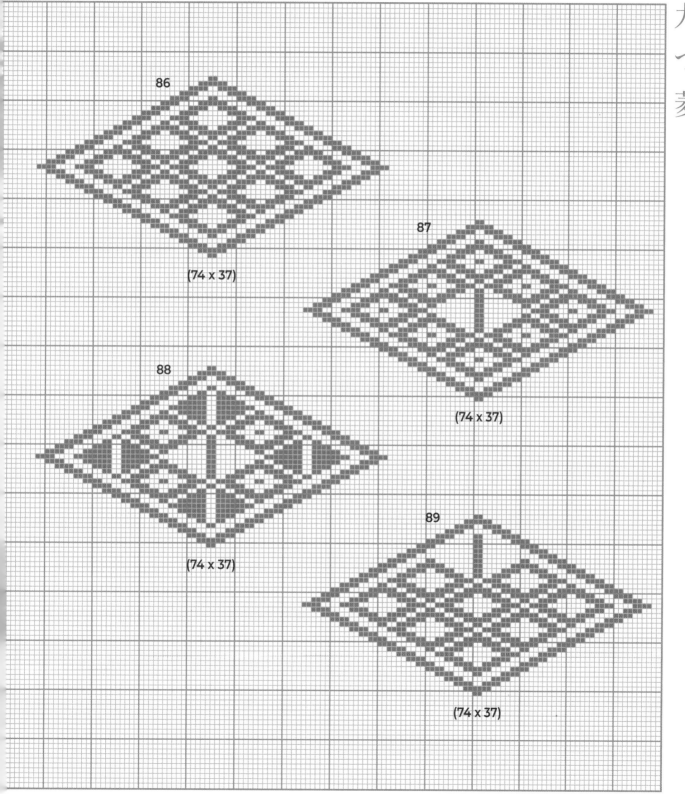

86

(74 x 37)

87

(74 x 37)

88

(74 x 37)

89

(74 x 37)

Hishizashi *Kokonotsubishi*

九つ菱

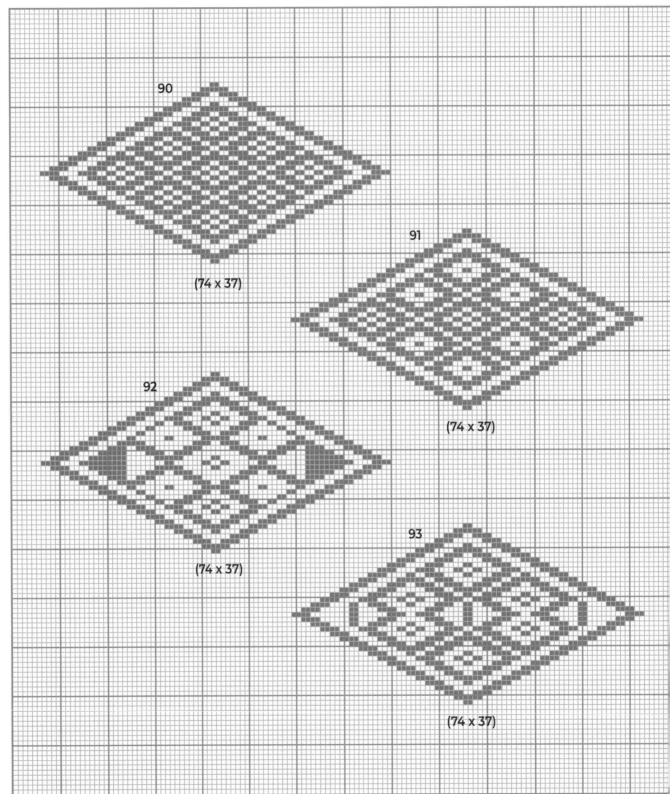

90 (74 x 37)

91 (74 x 37)

92 (74 x 37)

93 (74 x 37)

Hishizashi *Kokonotsubishi*

九つ菱

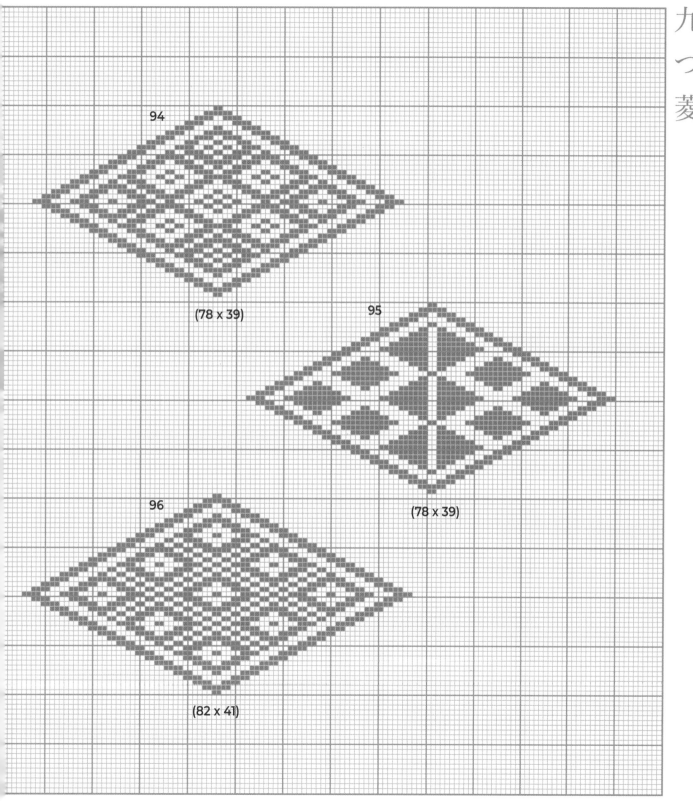

94

(78 x 39)

95

(78 x 39)

96

(82 x 41)

Hishizashi *Nashi no monko*

梨
の
紋
こ

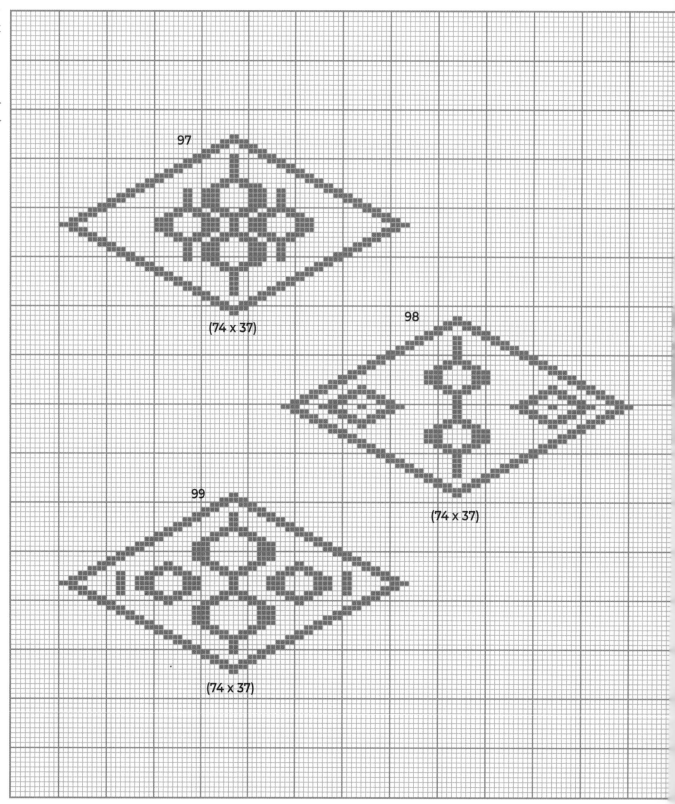

97

(74 x 37)

98

(74 x 37)

99

(74 x 37)

梨の紋こ

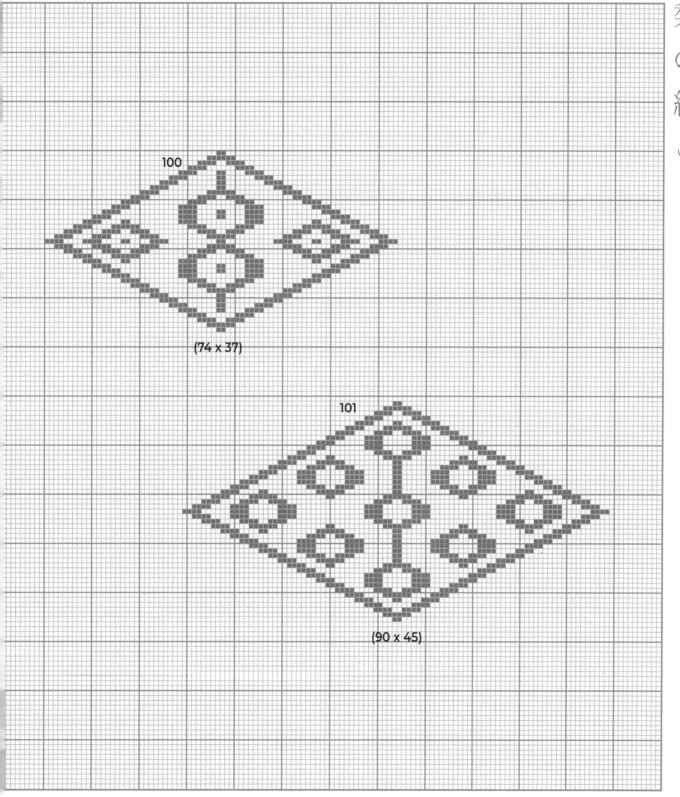

100

(74 x 37)

101

(90 x 45)

Hishizashi *Ougi no monko*

扇
の
紋
こ

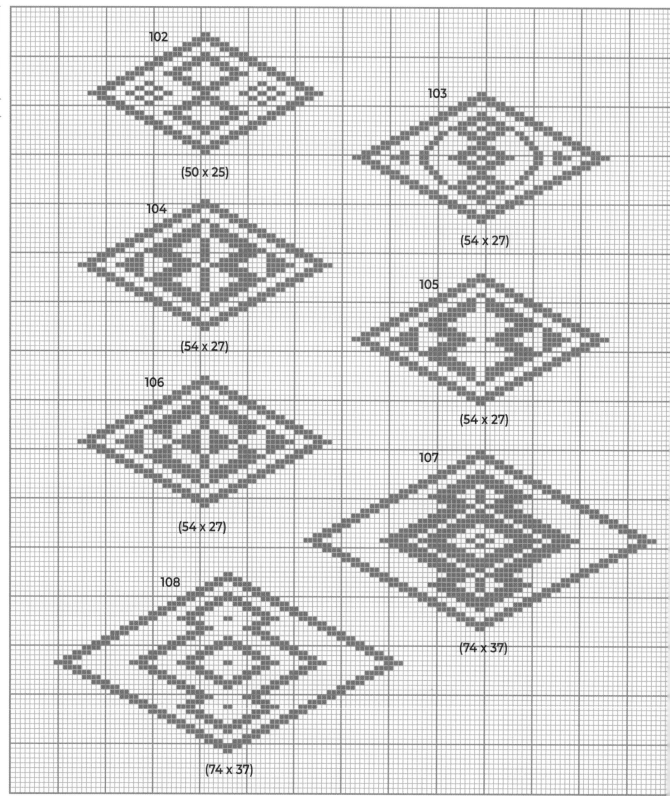

102
(50 x 25)

103
(54 x 27)

104
(54 x 27)

105
(54 x 27)

106
(54 x 27)

107
(74 x 37)

108
(74 x 37)

Hishizashi *Ougi no monko*

扇の紋こ

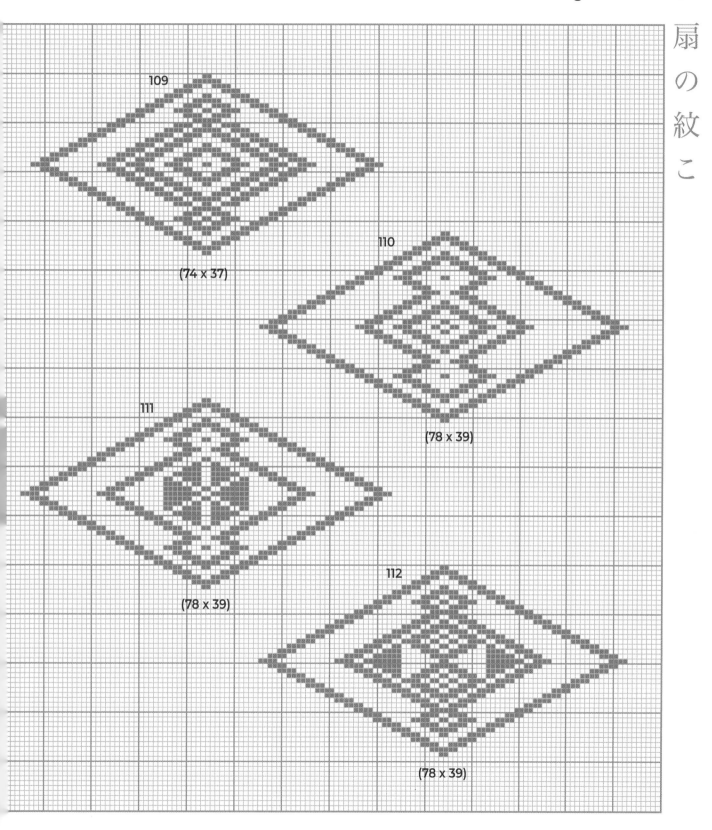

109
(74 x 37)

110
(78 x 39)

111
(78 x 39)

112
(78 x 39)

Hishizashi *Ishidatami*

石畳

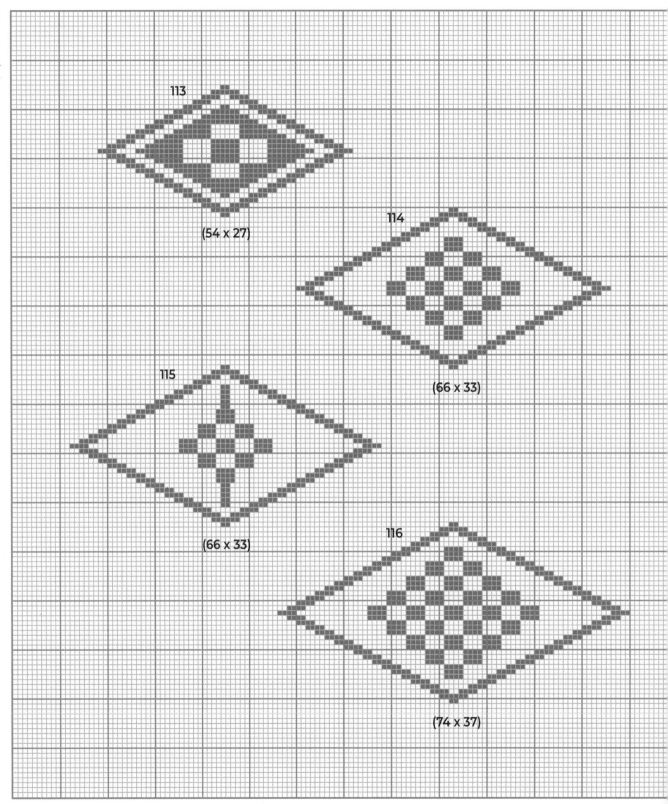

113
(54 x 27)

114
(66 x 33)

115
(66 x 33)

116
(74 x 37)

Hishizashi *Ajiro*

網代

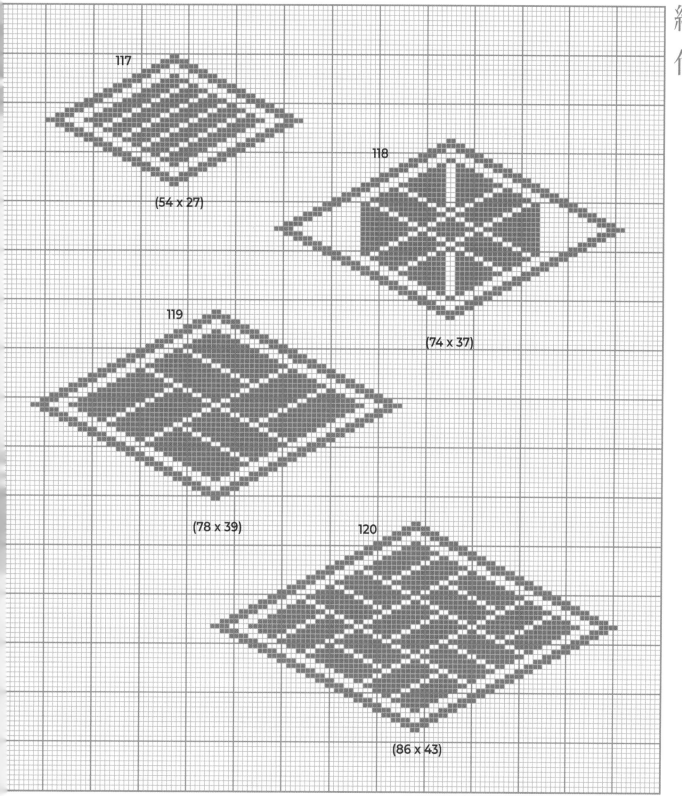

117

(54 x 27)

118

(74 x 37)

119

(78 x 39)

120

(86 x 43)

Hishizashi *Yanoha*

矢
の
羽

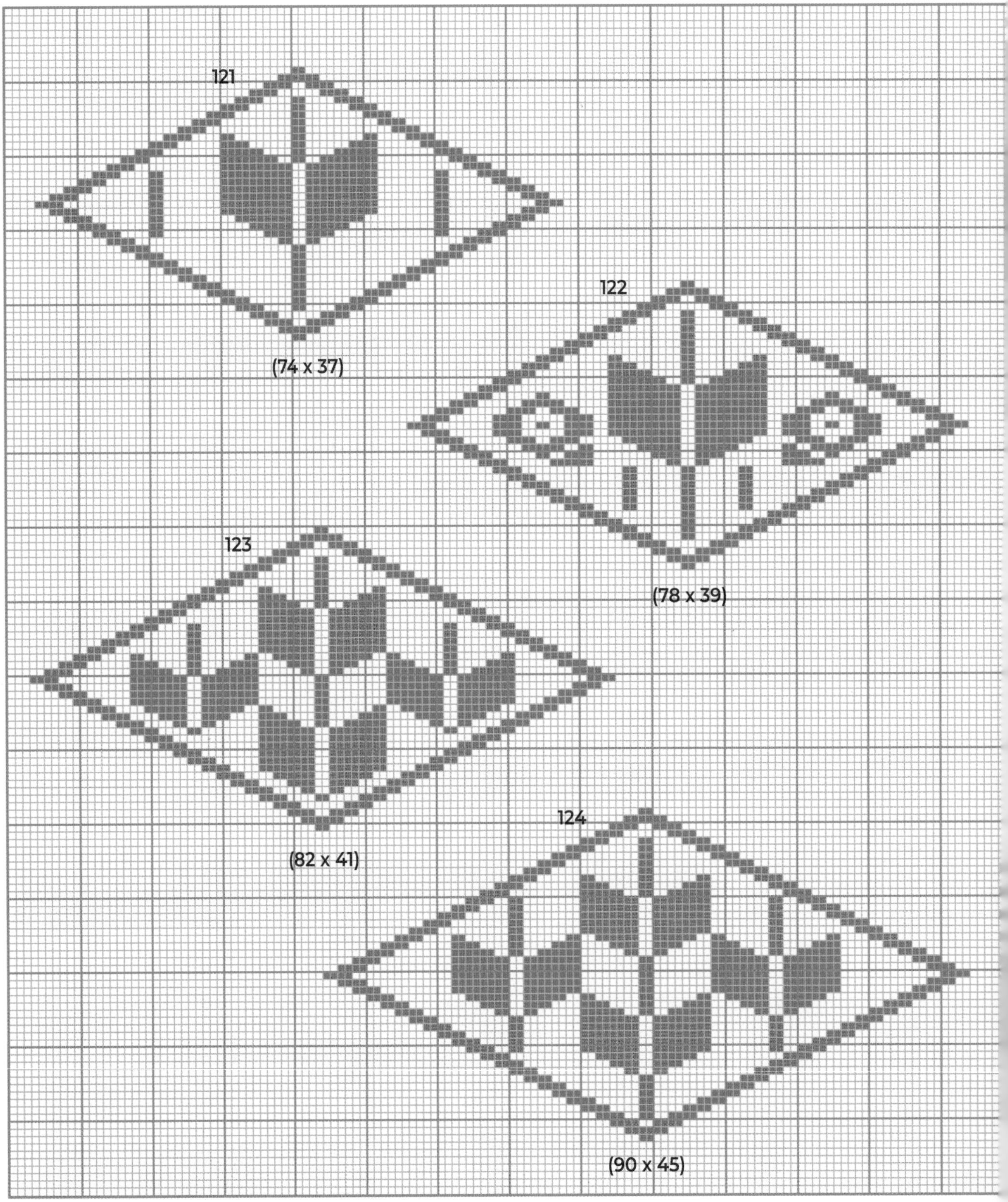

121

(74 x 37)

122

(78 x 39)

123

(82 x 41)

124

(90 x 45)

144

Hishizashi *Aishigemasu*

綾
杉
升

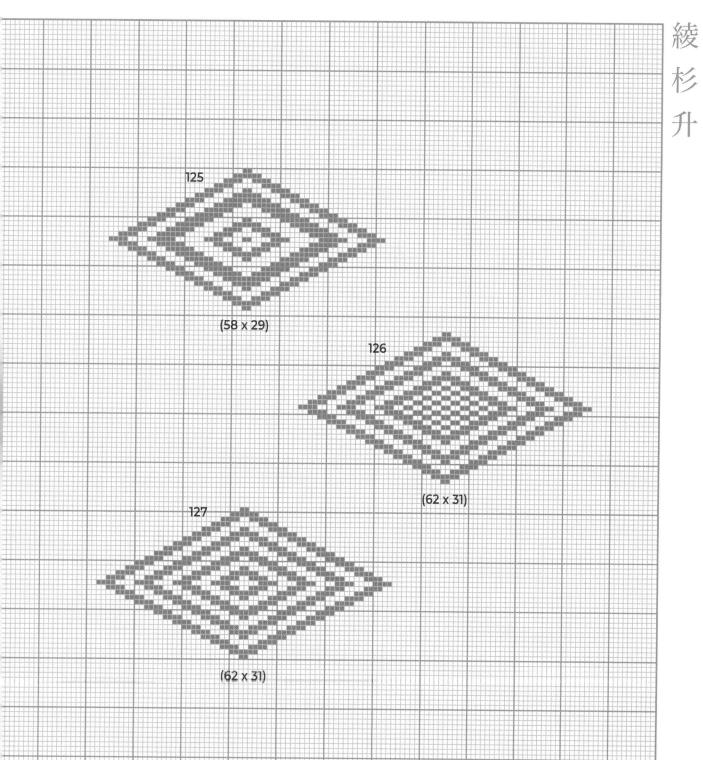

125

(58 x 29)

126

(62 x 31)

127

(62 x 31)

Hishizashi *Uma no managu*

馬のまなぐ

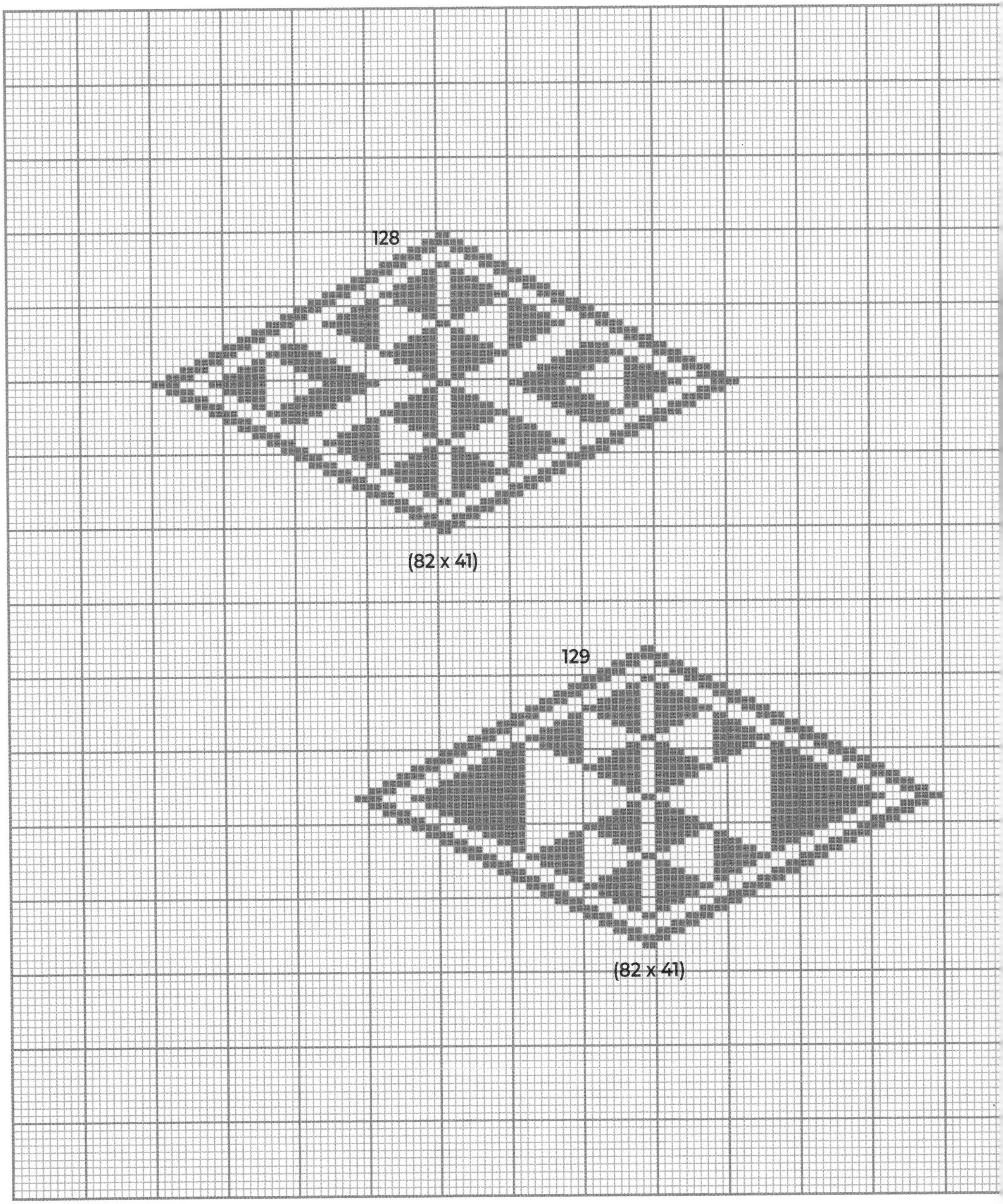

128

(82 x 41)

129

(82 x 41)

Hishizashi *Sobagarabishi*

蕎麦殻菱

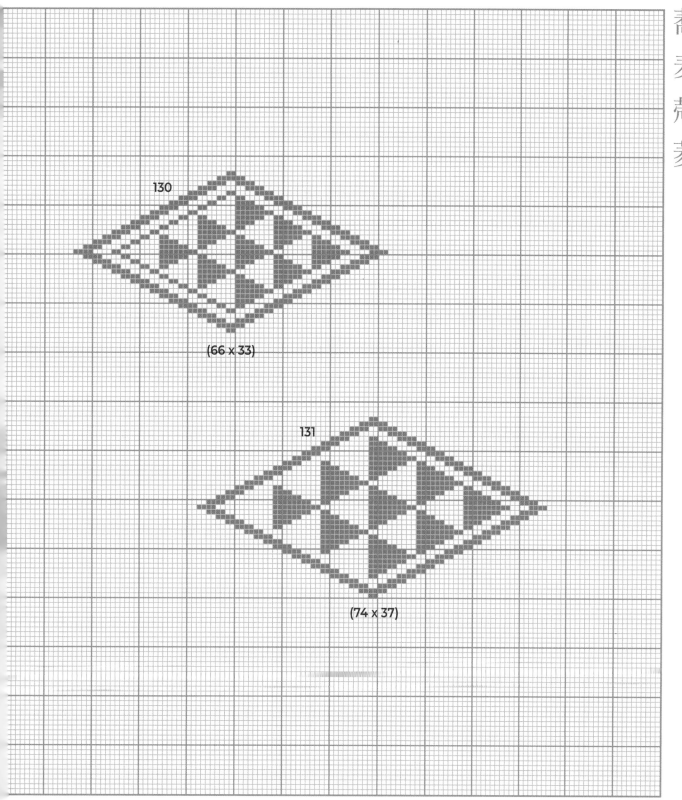

130

(66 x 33)

131

(74 x 37)

Hishizashi *Yanagi no ha* (willow leaf)

柳の葉

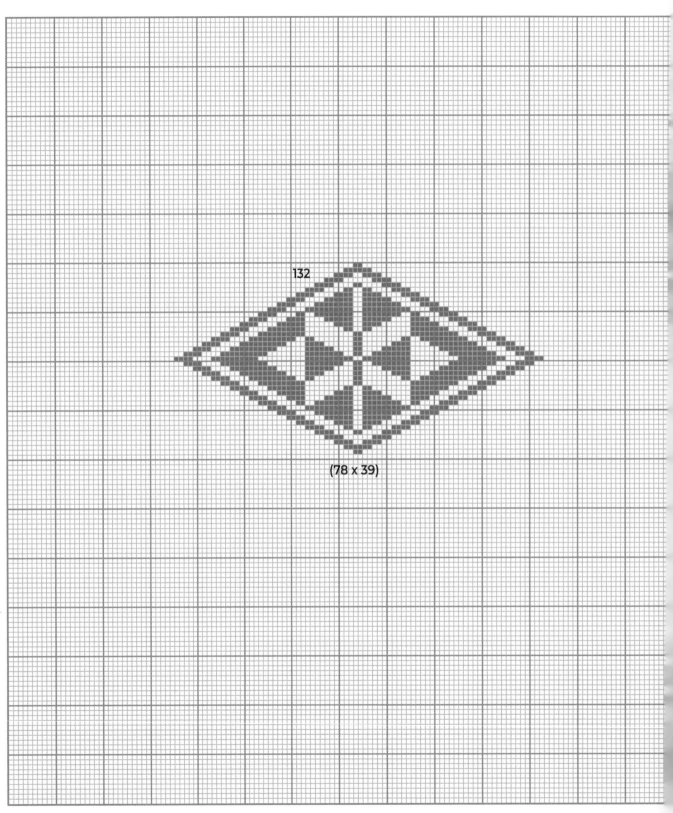

132

(78 x 39)

Hishizashi *Neko no managu*

猫のまなぐ

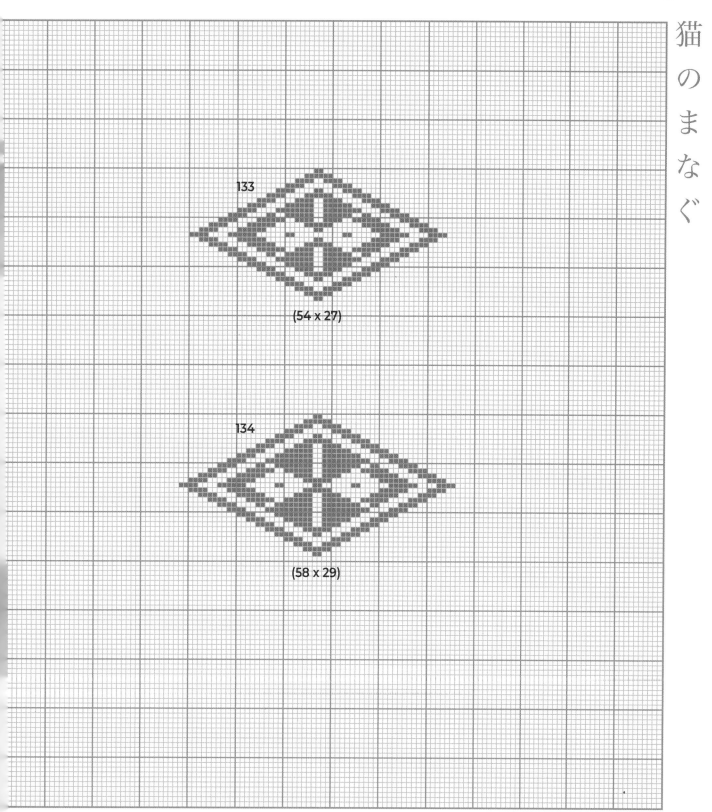

133

(54 x 27)

134

(58 x 29)

Hishizashi Others

その他型刺し

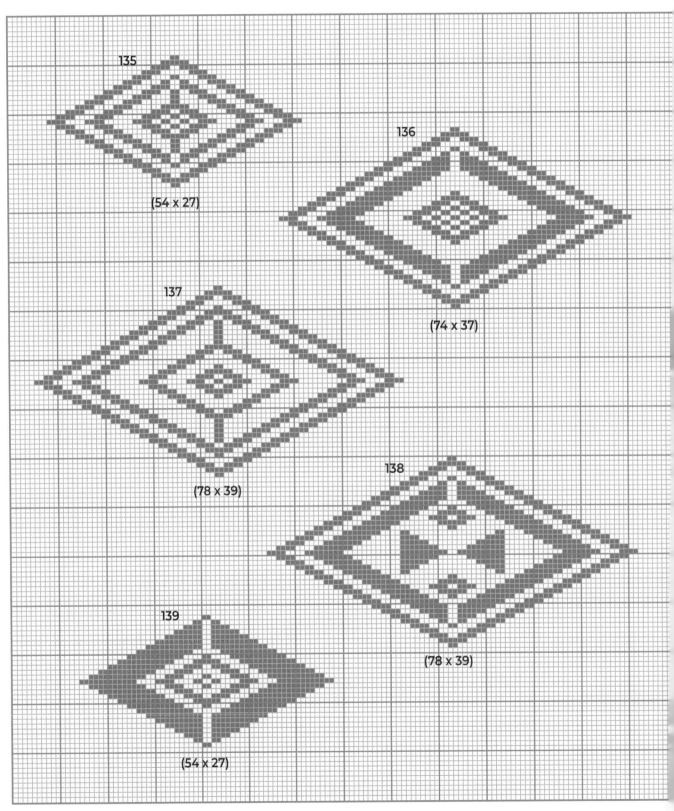

135
(54 x 27)

136
(74 x 37)

137
(78 x 39)

138
(78 x 39)

139
(54 x 27)

そ
の
他
型
刺
し

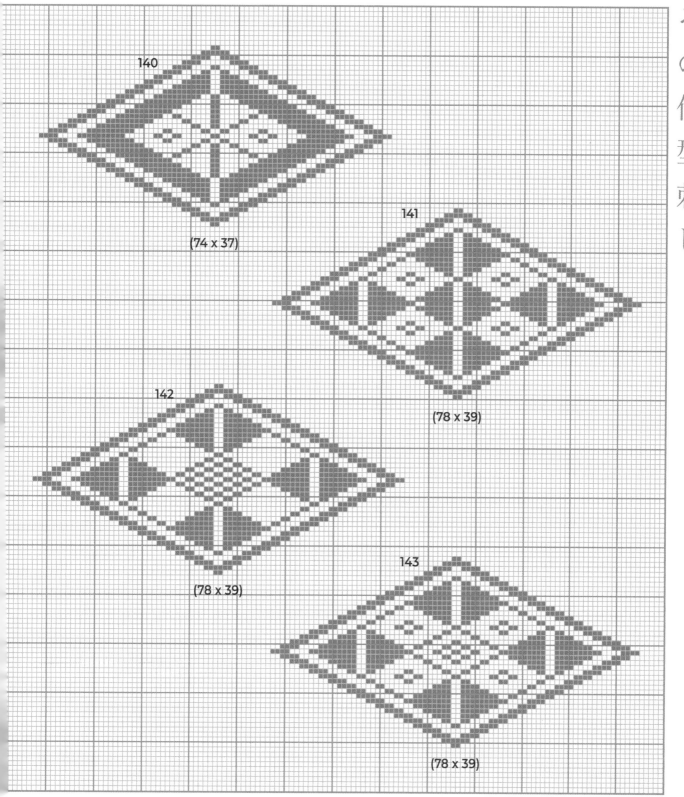

140

(74 x 37)

141

(78 x 39)

142

(78 x 39)

143

(78 x 39)

Hishizashi Others

その他型刺し

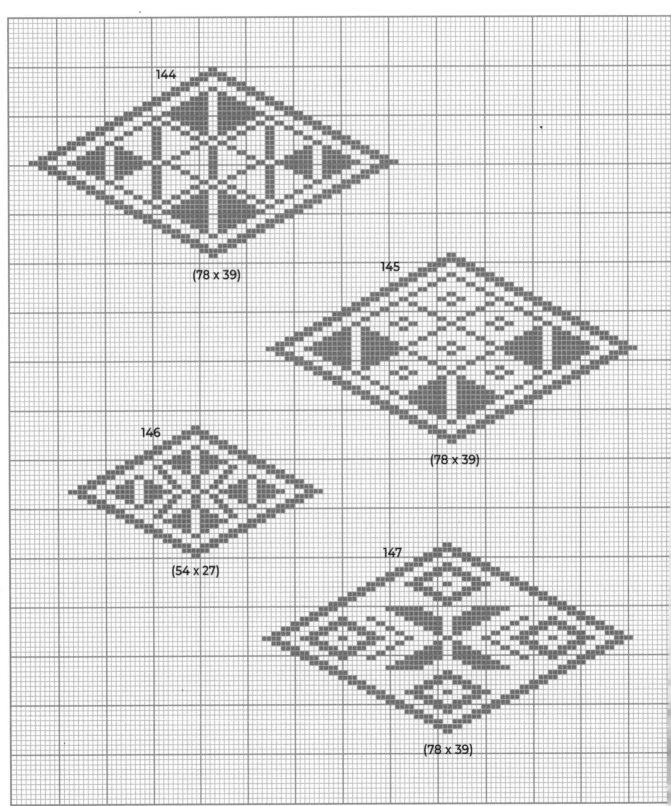

144

(78 x 39)

145

(78 x 39)

146

(54 x 27)

147

(78 x 39)

Hishizashi Others

その他型刺し

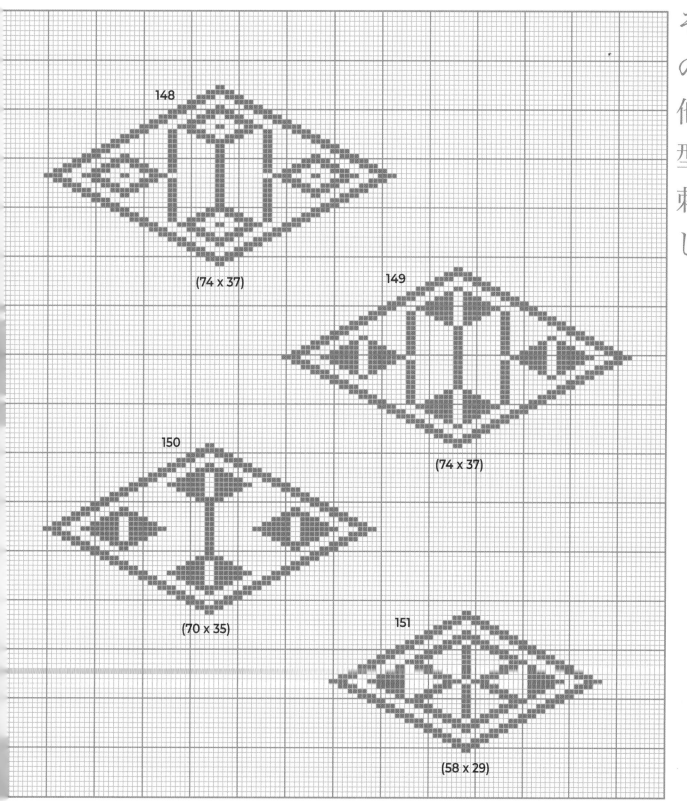

148

(74 x 37)

149

(74 x 37)

150

(70 x 35)

151

(58 x 29)

Hishizashi Others

その他型刺し

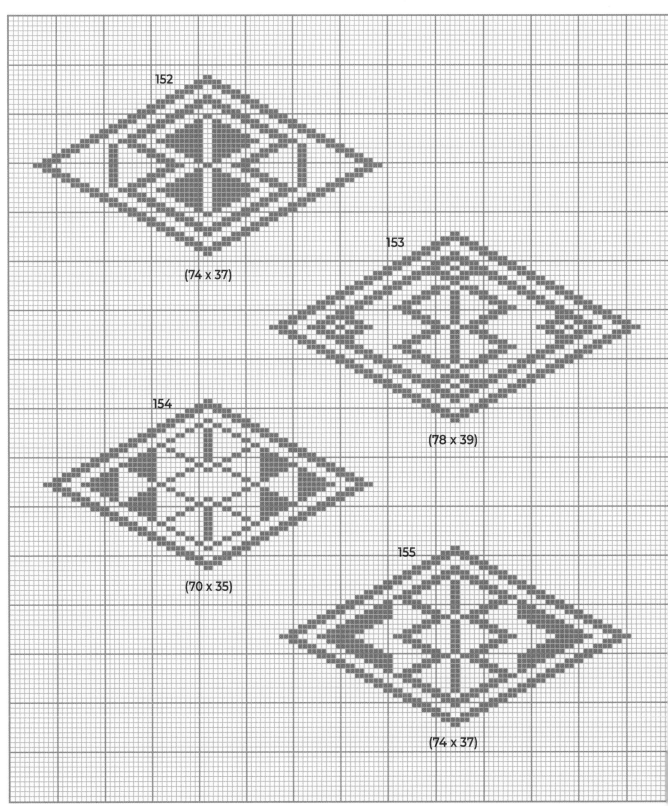

152

(74 x 37)

153

(78 x 39)

154

(70 x 35)

155

(74 x 37)

その他型刺し

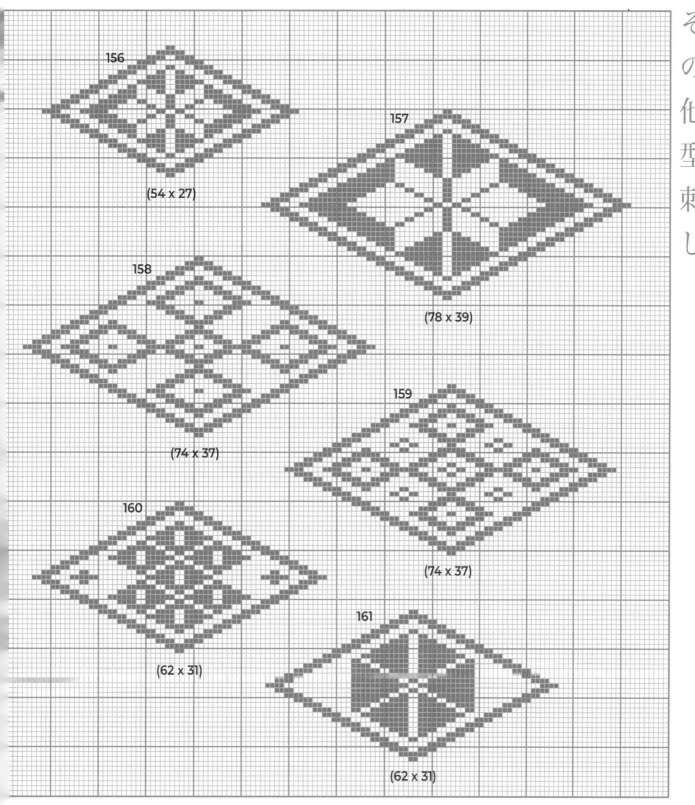

156

(54 x 27)

157

(78 x 39)

158

(74 x 37)

159

(74 x 37)

160

(62 x 31)

161

(62 x 31)

Hishizashi Others

その他型刺し

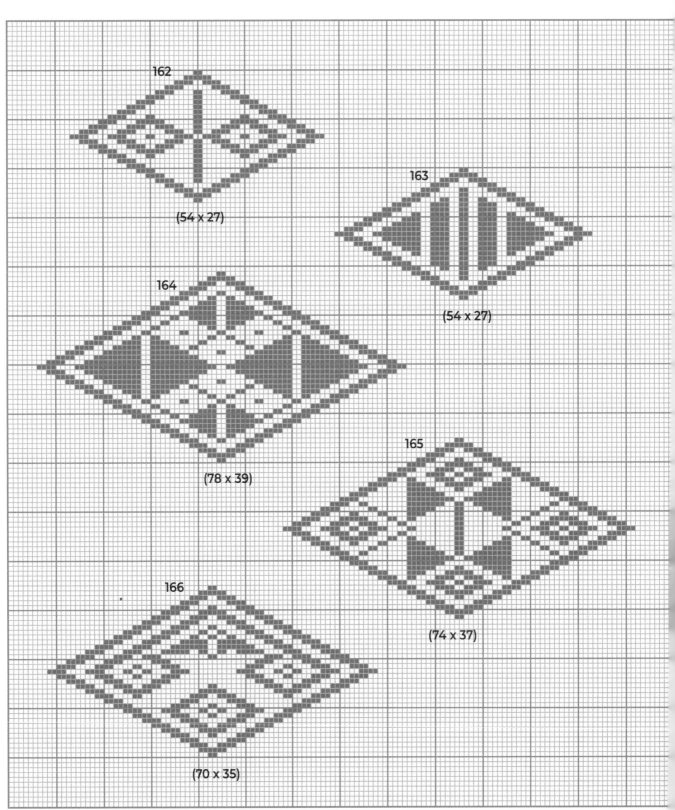

162

(54 x 27)

163

(54 x 27)

164

(78 x 39)

165

(74 x 37)

166

(70 x 35)

その他型刺し

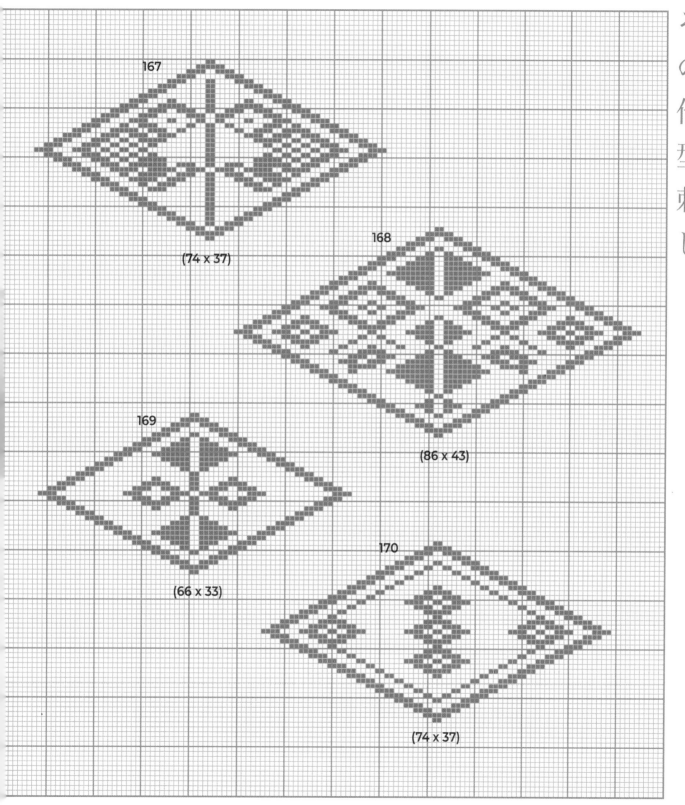

167
(74 × 37)

168
(86 × 43)

169
(66 × 33)

170
(74 × 37)

Hishizashi Continuous Patterns

地刺し

Hishizashi Continuous Patterns

地刺し

174

175

176

地刺し

177

178

179

地
刺
し

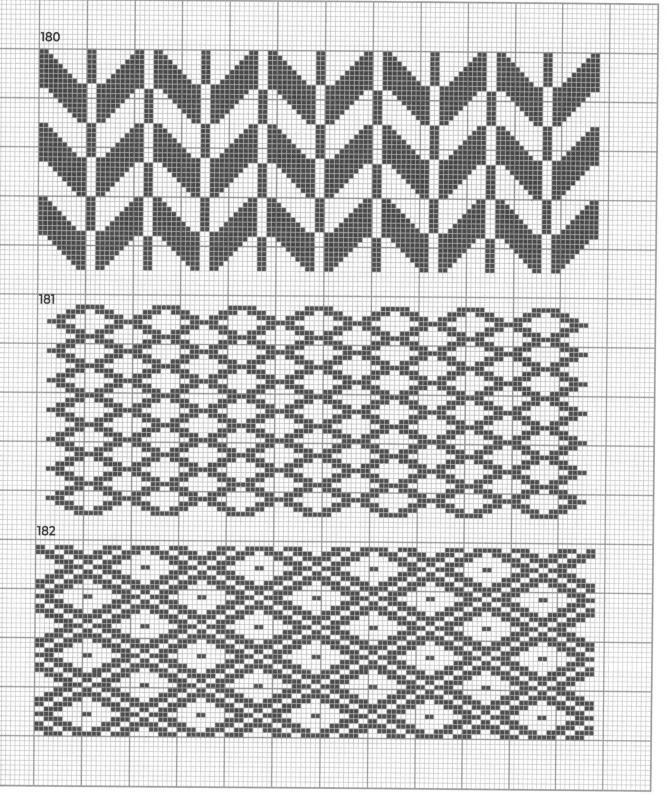

180

181

182

Hishizashi Continuous Patterns

地刺し

地刺し

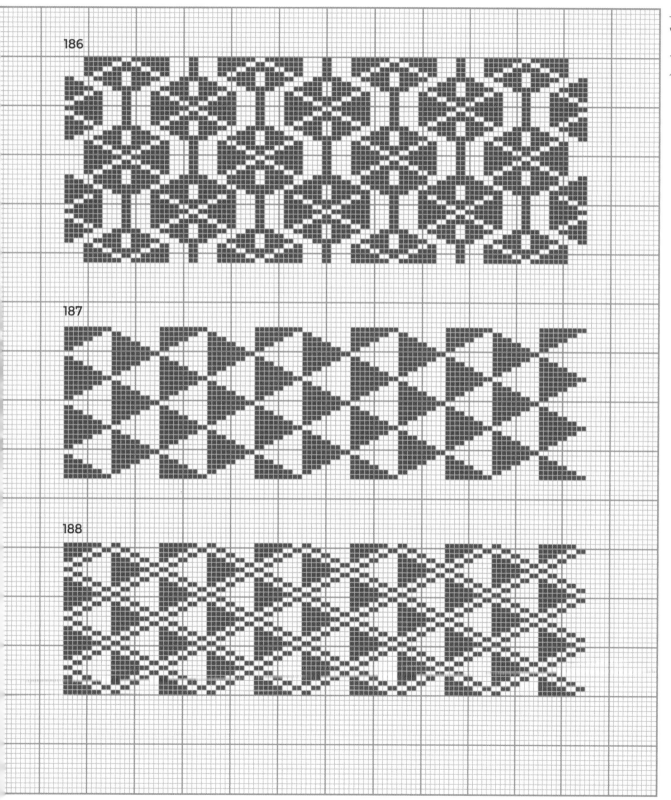

186

187

188

Hishizashi Continuous Patterns

地刺し

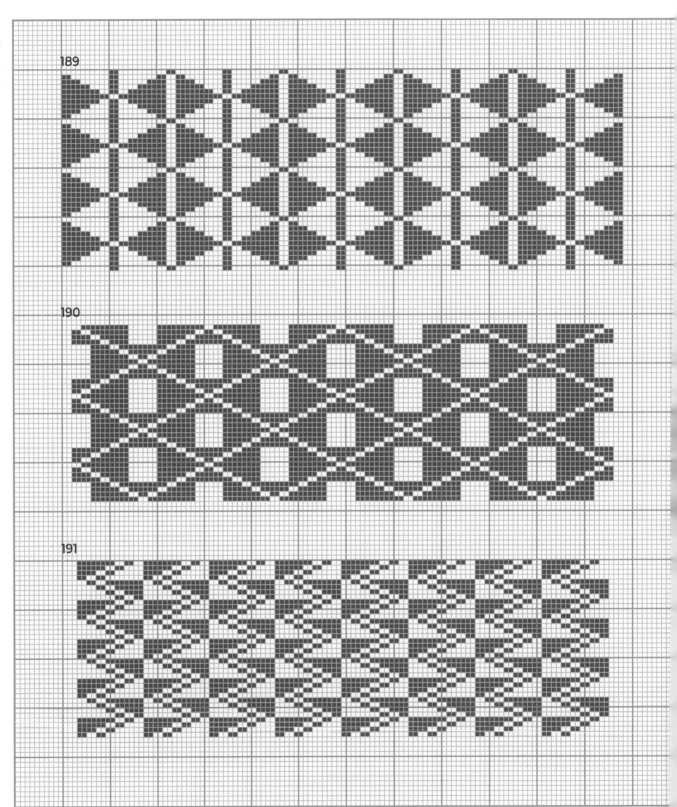

Hishizashi Continuous Patterns

地刺し

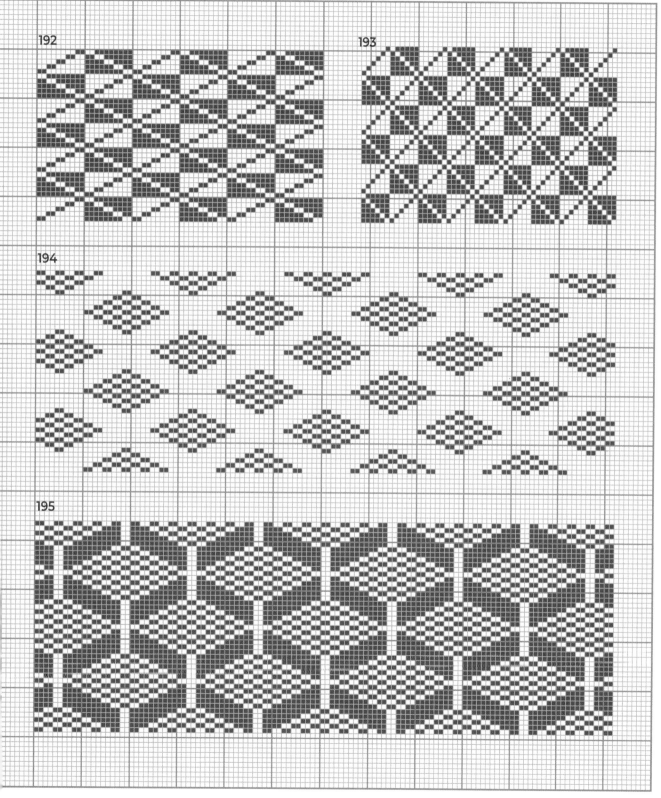

192

193

194

195

Hishizashi Continuous Patterns

地刺し

地刺し

199

200

Kogin Tapestry Complete

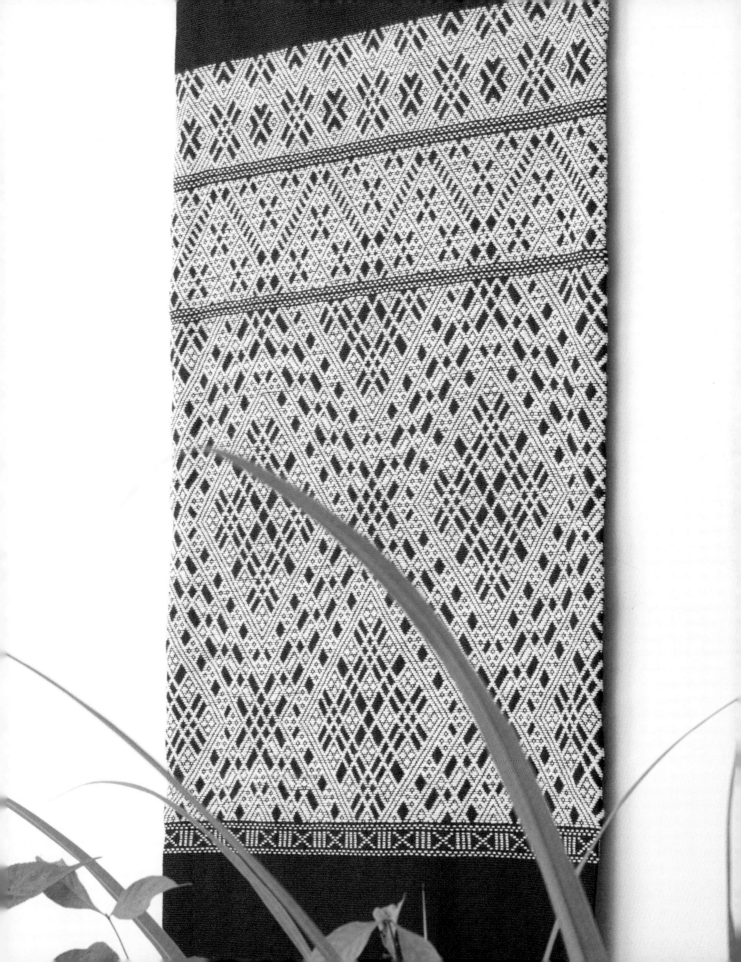

Kogin Tapestry Upper Left Quarter

Kogin Tapestry Upper Right Quarter

Kogin Tapestry Lower Left Quarter

Kogin Tapestry Lower Right Quarter

Hishizashi Tapestry Complete

Hishizashi Tapestry Upper Left Quarter

Hishizashi Tapestry Lower Left Quarter

Hishizashi Tapestry Lower Right Quarter

Bibliography

Hatta, Aiko, and Tomiko Suzuki. *Hishizashi no Giho* (Hishizashi embroidery techniques). Tokyo: Bijutsu Shuppansha, 1980.

Hirosaki Kogin Institute (supervised by). *Tsugaru Koginzashi*. Tokyo: Seibundo Shinkosha, 2013.

Kimura, Misao. *Kogin*. Tokyo: Fujingahosha, 1976.

Ogikubo, Kiyoko. *Kogin and Sashiko Stitch*. Kyoto: Kyoto Shoin, 1993.

Tanaka, Chuzaburo. *Nambu Tsuzure Hishizashi Moyoshu* (A Nambu Hishizashi pattern collection). Kitanomachisha, 197_.

Tanaka, Chuzaburo. *Zusetsu Michinoku no Kofu no Sekai* (An illustrated book of old clothes in Michinoku). Tokyo: Kawade Shobo Shinsha, 2009.

The Mingei 693 (September 2010). Japan Folk Crafts Association.

Tsugaru Kogin to Sashiko. Tokyo: INAX, 1998.

Yokoshima, Naomichi. *Tsugaru Kogin*. Tokyo: NHK, 1974.

Acknowledgments

First, I would like to express my deepest thanks to Schiffer Publishing and BlueRed Press for the opportunity to do this project.

Next, I would like to thank the many people who helped me in the creation of this book:
Masakazu Koga for taking all the photographs; Yukiko Hirano for styling; Hoki Graphics for the illustrations; William Polensky for all the English translation; Tori

Coffee, Autumn Kitijitsu, Nonaca Bakery, Cup of Tea Ensemble, Sangawa Antiques, and the Asahi family for providing the shooting locations and props.

Finally, special thanks to Satoko Tanaka and Kitanomachisha for permission to reproduce the patterns on behalf of the late Chuzaburo Tanaka. Without their understanding, this book of Sashiko counted embroidery would not have been possible.

About the Author

Keiko Sakamoto has been making and researching Japanese sashiko embroidery for the past 20 years. She learned Japanese needlework from a traditional kimono maker in Tokyo, but it was not until years later, when she was living in the American Midwest, that she picked her first sashiko project up again and finished it. Sakamoto has contributed to numerous publications on the subject in Japan. She runs the Aya Sashiko Studio. This book, her first in English, is part of her ongoing mission to collect information on the patterns, techniques, and materials used in kogin and hishizashi and to safeguard them for future generations. Sakamoto works to preserve the beauty of the traditional patterns while adapting them to modern tastes. She lives in a small town in the mountains of central Japan. www.aya-studio.com